HARVARD STUDIES
IN COMPARATIVE LITERATURE

VOLUME VIII

The Traditional Round Table in the Great Hall at Winchester

The rounde table at Wynchester beganne,
And there it ended, and there it hangeth yet.
John Hardyng, *Chronicle, ca.* 1457–64.

HARVARD STUDIES IN COMPARATIVE LITERATURE
VOLUME VIII

SPENSER AND THE TABLE ROUND

*A Study in the Contemporaneous Background
for Spenser's Use of the Arthurian Legend*

BY

CHARLES BOWIE MILLICAN
COLONEL, ARMY OF THE UNITED STATES, RETIRED
SOMETIME LECTURER IN ENGLISH IN THE AMERICAN UNIVERSITY

1967

OCTAGON BOOKS, INC.

New York

Reprinted 1967

by special arrangement with Harvard University Press

OCTAGON BOOKS, INC.
175 FIFTH AVENUE
NEW YORK, N. Y. 10010

LIBRARY OF CONGRESS CATALOG CARD NUMBER: 67–18776

Printed in U.S.A. by
NOBLE OFFSET PRINTERS, INC.
NEW YORK 3, N. Y.

TO

MARGUERITE

PREFACE TO THE
OCTAGON EDITION

MORE than thirty-five years have passed since this study was first published by the Harvard University Press, on March 16, 1932, as volume VIII of Harvard Studies in Comparative Literature, and I am now more than ever aware of my debt to Professor George Lyman Kittredge, to whom I dedicated the first edition. I also pay tribute to the memory of two more of my Harvard teachers, Professor Fred Norris Robinson and Professor Joshua Whatmough, who encouraged me in my research. I also must thank the Department of Comparative Literature of Harvard for approving and the Harvard University Press for permitting the republication of this volume. I am particularly grateful to my present publisher, who has kindly let me make a few revisions in the text. In the main, however, this reprint of the study is identical with the original.

The only additions that I have made to the text are references to Ralph Knevett of Oxnead and Lyng, Norfolk, as author of *A Supplement of the Faery Queene,* which I established in my article, "Ralph Knevett, Author of the *Supplement* to Spenser's *Faerie Queene,*" in *The Review of English Studies,* XIV (1938), pp. 44-52. Knevett's *Supplement* survives in University Library (Cambridge) MS. Ee.3.53, a holograph

that for a long time was attributed to Robert
Jegon of Buxton, Norfolk, who wrote for it a
commendatory poem, "Spencero Posthumo."
Because of my protracted military service in
World War II and in U.S. Military Government
in Germany after the war, I discontinued my
plan to publish an edition of Knevett's *Supplement* and turned over all of my material and
notes to Mr. Andrew Lavender, who prepared an
edition of the *Supplement* and submitted it (two
volumes in three, xiv + 1,246 pages) in partial
fulfillment of the requirements for the degree of
doctor of philosophy at New York University in
April 1955.

C.B.M.

DEERWOOD
MEEKER PARK, COLORADO
JULY 1, 1967

FROM THE ORIGINAL PREFACE

IN this study of Spenser and the Round Table
I have aimed to assist those readers who may
wish to look at *The Faerie Queene* in its historical perspective, and to this end I have attempted
to scan the Arthurian background of Tudor and
Stuart England. Original sources, some of them
of great rarity, have been consulted, and, for
obvious reasons, the antiquated and eccentric
spelling and punctuation have been preserved
in the numerous quotations, differences of type
being indicated by italics. It would have been
easier to modernize and regulate, but, after all,
the caprices and necessities of Renaissance
typography are, so to speak, a part of the exuber-
ance which surrounds *The Faerie Queene.*

Some details emerge from the mass of contemporary testimony that contribute, perhaps,
to our knowledge of Spenser's life. For my main
purpose, however, the gossip of the times is quite
as pertinent as biographical fact.

... The liberality of Harvard in granting me
both a Dexter Scholarship and a Sheldon Fellowship has brought about connections with scholars
in Wales and England, to three of whom I give
hearty thanks for their generous services in time
and attention—John Ballinger, Esq., of the
National Library of Wales, Aberystwyth, A. J.
Toppin, Esq., of the College of Arms, London,

and H. H. Evans, Esq., of the British Museum. For the use of manuscripts and rare books and for permission to make reproductions, I am grateful to Dr. A. S. W. Rosenbach and to the librarians of the Harvard College Library, the British Museum, the Bodleian, the Lambeth Palace Library, the College of Arms, the University Library, Cambridge, Queen's College, Oxford, the Huntington Library, the Pierpont Morgan Library, Columbia University, and the New York Public Library. . . . For enabling [the book] to see the light, I have to thank the Harvard University Press and a grant from the gift of the General Education Board to Harvard for the promotion of research in the Humanities. In every detail of the resulting volume Professor Kittredge has been an inspiration and a help in such a way that adequate expression of gratitude fails me. And there is another who receives inadequate thanks, she who has helped her husband conquer many a "dreadfull Dragon" since he entered the mountain fastnesses of Merionethshire to follow Prince Arthur in his quest of beauty through Faeryland.

C.B.M.

UNIVERSITY HEIGHTS
NEW YORK CITY
SEPTEMBER 1, 1931

CONTENTS

CONTENTS

ILLUSTRATIONS

In VVales, the true remnant of the auncient Brittons . . . .

SIR PHILIP SIDNEY, *The Defence of Poesie, ca. 1580–83.*

Ye Bryttish Poets, *Repeat in Royall Song,*
(*VVith waightie woords, vsde in King* Arthurs *daies*)
Th' Imperiall Stock, *from whence your* Queene *hath sprong;*
Enstall in verse your Princesse *lasting prayes:*
  Pencerddiaid, *play on Auncient Harp, and Crowde:*
  Atceiniaid, *sing her prayses pearcing lowd.*

MAURICE KYFFIN, *The Blessednes of Brytaine, or a*
Celebration of the Queenes Holyday, 1587.

No more our long-lost Arthur we bewail.
All-hail, ye genuine Kings, Britannia's Issue, hail !

THOMAS GRAY, *The Bard,* 1757.

SPENSER AND THE TABLE ROUND

CHAPTER I

INTRODUCTION

QUITE apart from the indebtedness of *The Faerie Queene* to the Arthurian romances and to the Arthurian material in the chronicles, there are facts in connection merely with Spenser's use of the Arthurian legend that are worthy of notice. Roger Ascham's famous words in *The Scholemaster*, "when Gods Bible was banished the Court, and *Morte Arthure* receiued into the Princes chamber," probably, according to Miss Lilian Winstanley, influenced Spenser's moral tone. "It was probably Ascham also," she says, "who dissuaded or helped to dissuade Spenser from making much use of Malory's *Morte d'Arthure*." [1] Miss Winstanley calls attention, furthermore, to the stress that Spenser "lays upon Arthur and, in various portions of his poem, upon the Arthurian descent of the Tudors." She continues: "The claim of Arthurian descent involved the claim that Britain had, at one time, been an empire; hence it formed an invaluable foundation for the Imperial idea and was used to support the Tudor claim to supremacy over the whole island, including Wales and Scotland; moreover it was an exceedingly useful weapon against the Papal supremacy since it involved the claim that Britain had once been independent of Rome." [2] The use of Arthurian material in pageantry, and its probable effect on Spenser, mentioned as early as Thomas Warton and elaborated by Professor Edwin Greenlaw, has been observed in the case of Leicester's entertainment for Elizabeth at Kenilworth in 1575.[3] Professor Greenlaw suggests that Spenser himself may have been present at Leicester's revels.[4] He also suggests that the historical allegory of *The Faerie Queene* may have been influenced by the attack which was levelled at Polydore Vergil,[5] and he lays emphasis on John Leland's and Richard Robinson's exaltation of "Briton as against Saxon claims to merit as the founders of all that was great in England." "Historical primitivism" is his term for the spirit "that led to the exaltation of the Tudors as restorers of the pristine British glory, and that motivates Spenser's *Faerie Queene*." [6] Legouis, with the characteristic grace of his imagination, would believe that young Edmund [7] saw the coronation of Elizabeth on January 15, 1559: "Si l'enfant ne vit pas le couronnement," yet "il put assister au pageant des Sept Champions de la Chrétienté et à celui du Roi Arthur et de ses Chevaliers. Sa jeune imagination en fut marquée pour la vie." [8] But only a few more suggestions have been made, and

little else has been done to orient Spenser in the
Arthurian interests of Tudor Englishmen.

The more we read in the literature and life of
Tudor England, the more we come to know that
especially its florescence in the reign of Elizabeth
was a period when Englishmen made the strongest
attempt, among other things, to realize the impact
of a national past upon their own life and thought.
Of that attempt, the obvious Arthurian ferment in
connection with the Tudors is not the least significant phase.[9] Quite as much as Spenser's scholarly
training and his nationality, the age in which he
lived is fundamental to the understanding of his
art. Thus writes Professor W. L. Renwick: "The
promotion of Spenser from Clerk of Degrees and
Recognisances to the Irish Court of Chancery to
Clerk of the Council of Munster may have meant
that he had more or less time to spend on *The
Faerie Queene*, but made no difference to the subject, the plan, or the style of the great poem. The
chain of accidents which led to his meeting with
Raleigh culminated in *Colin Clouts Come Home
Again*, but did not make that poem a pastoral." [10]
Professor Renwick writes with sound judgment,
and there are aspects of the Arthurian legend both
in England and on the Continent, heretofore unre-
lated to Spenser, which unquestionably affected
him both in the very choice of subject and in the

materials he came to use. Spenser, who is of the
Elizabethans Elizabethan, articulates the period in
which he lived, and his journey to Camelot is as
intensely Elizabethan as Ralegh's expeditions to
Virginia or Drake's adventures on the Spanish
Main.

CHAPTER II

THE EARLY TUDOR PERIOD

Mîl yw o Wynedd, wr moliannus,
Adar a tharw o waed Arthurus;

. . . .

Oddyna ydd â drwy 'r ddawnus vreniniaeth,
Y ceidw lywodraeth Cadwaladrus.

Evo yw 'r atteg hir o Vrutus.
LEWIS GLYN COTHI, I'r Brenin Harri VII, ca. 1485.

Optima spes rerum maestos solata Britaños
Sorte reuicturum promisit, & omine laeto
Arturum, obscuro lucem qui redderet orbi.
Tempus adest. Victor prodit rediuiuus in auras.
JOHN LELAND, Arturius Rediuiuus, 1544.

IN ITS broadest sense, Spenser's use of the Arthurian legend is a feature of the antiquarian movement which derived its impetus from the vigorous nationalistic policy of Henry VII. In the preface to his edition of Malory's *Morte d'Arthur*, published in 1485, the year of Henry's accession, William Caxton gave expression to the national feeling that centered about the figure of Arthur,

the moost renomed crysten kyng/ Fyrst and chyef of the thre best crysten and worthy/ kyng Arthur/ whyche ought moost to be remembred emonge vs englysshe men tofore al other crysten kynges/ [1]

But the reverence for Arthur went beyond his recognition as the greatest of Christian kings. First and foremost, Arthur was a British king, an emperor, who, on the authority of Geoffrey of Monmouth, had extended the empire of Britain beyond the Alps and the Pyrenees. Also according to Geoffrey, after his last battle Arthur had been borne to the island of Avalon for the healing of his wounds, and, during the centuries that followed, the notion had become more and more fixed in the minds of the Britons as they retreated before the Saxons that the Boar of Cornwall should one day restore them to their lawful sovereignty. According to Geoffrey again, Cadwalader ap Cadwallon, the last king of the Britons, had given up a final attempt to reconquer the island because an angel had revealed to him that God willed the Britons should reign no more in Britain until the time should be fulfilled according to the *Prophecies of Merlin*. Wherefore the loyal Britons bided their time and doggedly resisted the attempt of the Angevin dynasty to make merchandise of Arthur and dominate Wales. In a way, the untimely death of the hapless young Arthur Plantagenet, "desideratus gentibus," put a definite end to Henry II's earlier desire to unite the island.[2] By the time of the Wars of the Roses it was especially the Welsh who kept alive the hope which Edward I had attempted to destroy officially in 1282 by mounting the head of Llewelyn ap Griffith "vpon one of the highest turrets of the Towre of *London*,"[3] and looked forward to the day when Arthur should return, if not in person, then in a Welsh claimant for the English throne.[4] Thus Henry Tudor, Earl of Richmond, "who by his grandfather *Owen Tuder* descended out of *Wales*,"[5] came to be welcomed as a Briton Messiah. The Tudor interest in Arthur, therefore, was something more than an antiquarian revival of a glorious *past* of British empire. It was a revival, to be sure, but it was a revival enhanced by the belief that in the Welsh blood of Henry of Richmond the very blood of Arthur had returned to a glorious *present* of British empire. The foundation for the belief was brought about by the marriage of Owen ap Meredith ap Tudor — a Welsh gentleman who was "brought furth and come of the noble lignage, and aūcient lyne of Cadwaleder, the laste kyng of the Brytons "[6] — with Catherine of Valois, daughter of Charles VI of France and widow of Hal of Agincourt.[7]

Through his mother, Owen Tudor was cousin to Owen Glendower, and it was probably through Glendower's son, who entered the service of Henry V, that Owen Tudor first came to the English court. Early in the reign of Henry VI he became clerk of the wardrobe to Catherine, and they soon lived together as man and wife. In 1427–28 an act was passed making it a serious offence to marry a queen-dowager without the consent of the king and his council, but Owen and Catherine were reported to be already married. At any rate, whether the marriage, legally or not, ever took place, from their union Owen and Catherine had three sons, Edmund, Jasper, and Owen, and at least one daughter.[8] The Tudor line was obviously spurious, but Henry VI recognized his half-brother, young Edmund of Hadham, and knighted him on December 15, 1449. On March 6, 1453, Edmund was created Earl of Richmond and premier earl, and in 1455 he married Margaret Beaufort, great-granddaughter of John of Gaunt and Catherine Swynford.[9] From this union sprang a posthumous son, Henry, Earl of Richmond, who was born in Pembroke Castle, South Wales, on January 28, 1457, and who, owing to the fact that the Beauforts had been legitimated by Richard II in 1397, and that the legitimation had been confirmed by Henry IV, was soon recognized as having a Lancastrian claim to the English throne.[10]

After the battle of Tewkesbury (May 4, 1471), which resulted in the butchery of Edward of Westminster, Prince of Wales, Henry of Richmond became the chief claimant of the Lancastrians, for

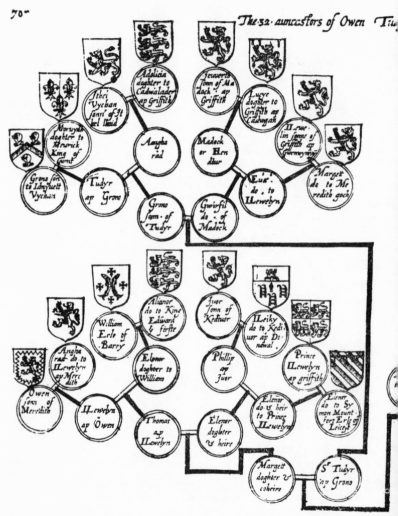

A Genealogy of Owen Tudor in George Owen Harry's *Genealo*

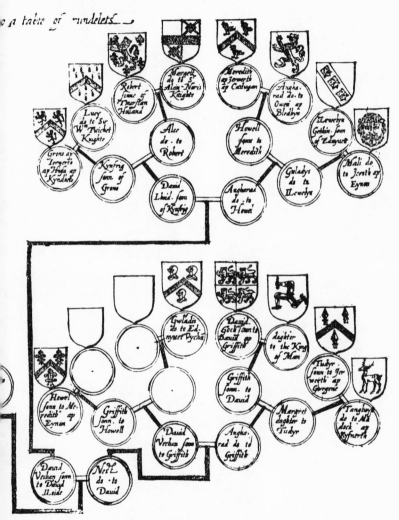

o a table of rundelets

Robert some of Thurstan Holland
Margett do to S Alein Noris Knighte
Meredith ap Ierworth ap Cadugan
Angharad do. to Owen ap Bledhyn

Lucy do to Sr Wm Twichet Knighte
Alce do. to Robert
Howell sonn to Meredith
Llewelyn Gethin sonn of Llanvirt

Grono ap Ierworth ap Hoза ap Kynduet
Kynvrig sonn of Grono
David Lhuit sonn of Kynvrig
Angharad do. to Howel
Guladys do. to Llewelyn
Mali do to Ierith ap Eynon

Gwladis do to Ed. mynet Vychā
David Goch sonn to David Griffith
daghter to the King of Man

Howel sonn to Meredith ap Eynon
Griffith sonn to Howell
Griffith sonn. to David
Tudyr sonn to Ierworth ap Gorgene

David Vechan sonn to Griffith
Angharad do to Griffith
Margret daghter to Tudyr
Tanghey do to Mil Jack ap Kynerth

David Vechan sonn to David Lhoide
Nest do. to David

d Mighty Monarch, Iames, 1604. (British Museum C.64.d.12.)

Henry VI was already in the Tower, where he died on the day of Edward IV's reëntry into London. Jasper Tudor, who had also been knighted by Henry VI and created Earl of Pembroke, took charge of his nephew and escaped to Brittany. In 1483 Henry Stafford, Duke of Buckingham, advanced the claim of the young earl to the throne, but the first attempt was unsuccessful, and Buckingham lost his head. Henry, without landing, returned to Brittany to wait until the time was fully ripe to unhorse Richard III. Fortune smiled upon another attempt, and in August, 1485, the march of the twenty-eight-year-old Henry from Milford Haven through Wales to meet Richard was a veritable triumph.[11] "When the Welshmen were put in mind, that (being the son [*i.e.*, grandson] of Owen *Tuthar*) hee was of their owne bloud, . . . they flocked vnto him,"[12] and, according to one story, the Welsh actually hailed their champion as Owen rather than Henry. Henry was greeted as the "Black Bull" and the "Bull of Mona," and a wave of prophetic literature foretold his success.[13] Saint David was called upon to lend his spiritual aid, and it was a triumphal gathering on August 22 that carried to victory at Market Bosworth the banners of the "dōne kowe," "S. George," and the Red Dragon of Cadwalader, "a red firye dragō beaten vpō white and green sarcenet."[14] Granted that Henry was little more than "the proscribed grandson of a Welsh squire,"[15] yet the Welsh bards broke into song, relating him to Brutus, Arthur, and Cadwalader. Thus sings Lewis Glyn Cothi[16] in his ode *I'r Brenin Harri VII* (*ca.* 1485),[17] which was written in commemoration of Henry's victory:

DUW dodes *fortun*, do; doded hirhoedl
I'r *King* Harri seithved;
Da y gŵyr wedi gwared
Dỳnu 'r groes a'i dwyn i'r Gred.

Trwy Gred tair saled vu 'n seilio *siasau*
Sywlius Sesar Penvro;
Tarw Mon â i'r tir y mỳno,
Troia vawr anturiai vo.

Evo iarll Penvro rhag pob *hort* a dig,
Siaspar Dug o Bedfort;
Ei nai ev aeth â'r hen vort
Gròn hapus, wrth gaer Newport.

Milfort, a Newport, a gwlad Non! dyn hir,
Dan Harri a'i goron;
Mae'r Nordd, pum rhan y Werddon,
A Deau 'n fest dan ei fòn.

Ei ddwy fòn linon drwy 'r Vel ynys aeth,
A sêl Uthr ac Emrys;
Da o'r dwr, i dir dyrys,
Droi rhàn o Dewdwr a Rhys.

. . . . . .

Mìl yw o Wynedd, wr moliannus,
Adar a tharw o waed Arthurus;
Goludawg vrenin o gorf Gwladus Ddu;
A deryw dỳnu o Dardanus.

Aeth a'r *hêt* alawnt air Twlius,
A mawr lawenydd gair Merlinius;
A gwr ydyw sy gariadus a theg,
A'i wyr yw deuddeg anrhydeddus.

Henri o Beli nid govalus,
Henri yw brenin yn nhir Brenius;
Hevyd trwy y byd gwybodus yr aeth,
Hwn a gwroliaeth hen Garolus.

Llin o Garedig a llaw 'n gariadus,
Llin gwr o nawosgl llin Gorineus;
Llin Dardan tarian tawrus tair talaith,
Llin Troia eilwaith a llin Troilus.

.   .   .   .   .   .

Y deyrnas isod drwy enw Siesus
Sy i'r *King* Harri rhyswr cynghorus;
Oddyna ydd â drwy 'r ddawnus vreniniaeth,
Y ceidw lywodraeth Cadwaladrus.

Evo yw 'r atteg hir o Vrutus,
Ev wedi Selyv o waed Silius;
O ddynion Troia, lwyddiannus vonedd,
Ac o ais Gwynedd ac Ysganus.

O Ysganus ais Gynan
Yn breiniwyd ein brenin;
O Droia vawr draw i Von
Dewr a phert draw yw 'r fortun.

Professor Joshua Whatmough has kindly furnished the prose translation which follows:

God has given good fortune to King Henry VII; assuredly he has; let him grant also long life; well does he know how to take away the Cross, after deliverance, and bring it to Christendom.

Through Christendom three helmets have waged campaigns, the Julius Cæsar of Pembroke; the Bull of Mona goes to whatever land he chooses; he would venture great Troy itself.

He, the great Pembroke, in spite of every calumny and wrath, Jasper, Duke of Bedford; his nephew took possession of the merry Round Table of yore, close to the fort of Newport.

Milford, Newport, and the land of Pembroke; a tall hero, upholding Henry and his crown; the North, five provinces of Ireland, and the South are safe and sound under his rule.

His two ashen spears have traversed Britain, and the seal of Uther and Emrys; well it is that Tudor and Rhys have turned for their portion from the sea to the land. . . .

The beast from North Wales, a man of renown, birds and bull of the blood of Arthur; a wealthy king descended from Gladys Ddu; traced back to Dardanus.

He has won the heat of the greyhound according to the word of Tullius, and the great joy predicted by Merlin; he is kindly and fair, and his men are twelve honorable ones.

Henry heeds not Beli; Henry is king in the land of Brennus; also his fame has spread through the learned world like that of Charlemagne.

His line is from Ceredig of kindly hand; the lineage of a man of nine branches, the line of Corineus, the line of Dardan, the shield of Taurus, three provinces, the line of Troy, and the line of Troilus. . . .

By the name of Jesus, the kingdom belongs to King Henry, a wise champion; thence will it come to pass by his wise rule that he will keep up the government of Cadwalader.

He is the tall pillar from Brutus; he next to Selyf is from Silvius; from the men of Troy, a prosperous race, from the bosom of Gwynedd, from Ascanius.

From Ascanius, the bosom of Cynan, has our king received his privileges; from great Troy yonder to Mona; fine and fair is the fortune.

Nor was Welsh jubilation over Henry merely that of an occasional outburst of heraldic poetry penned in the fever of victory. It is a fact of sober history that "because Henry was sprung from Welsh princes, the Welsh could regard him as their rightful king and no mere descendant of their conqueror," [18] and they sincerely considered him not only the possessor of the iron crown of Britain and the restorer of Arthur and the line of ancient British kings, but also "the first Brittish King" of England.[19] The position of the Northwallian Henry over all Wales was strengthened because of his descent from Rhys ap Tudor, the famous hero of South Wales in the eleventh century.[20] From the outset the Tudor dynasty was popular in Wales, and Henry's greatest contribution to the spirit of British nationalism and empire was himself.

In Henry's coronation procession at Westminster on October 30, 1485, members of great families bore a banner displaying the Red Dragon of Cadwalader. Welsh enthusiasm became more spirited on January 18, 1486, when Henry married Elizabeth of York, the daughter of Edward IV, who traced her descent from Llewelyn ap Iorwerth, or the Great.[21] When she was crowned, a barge came forth from Greenwich "wherin was ordeynede a great red Dragon spowting Flamys of Fyer into

Temmys." [22] Henry himself looked with pride upon his descent from Owen Tudor, and replaced his grandmother's tomb erected by Henry VI in the Lady Chapel of Westminster Abbey by another monument which gave due reference to her marriage with Owen Tudor and to Owen's lineage.[23] Feeling that the pedigree of Owen was called in question,[24] Henry, soon after his accession, appointed a commission to make an official report on his Cymric genealogy:

> There was a commission at this time directed from king *Henrie* the seauenth, to the Abbot of *Lhan Egwest*, Doctor *Owen Poole* chanon of *Hereford*, and *Iohn King*, harold, to make inquisition concerning the parentage of the said *Owen*, who comming to *Wales*, trauelled in that matter, and vsed the helps of Sir *Iohn Leyaf*, *Guttyn Owen Bardh*, *Gruffyth ap Lhewelyn ap Euan Vachan*, and others in the search of the Brytish or *Welsh* bookes of petigrées, out of the which they drew his perfect genelogie from the ancient kings of *Brytaine* and the Princes of *Wales*, and so returned their commission: which returne is extant at this daie to be séene.[25]

The report of the commission reads in part:

> Of which *Brute* [*i. e.*, "*Brutus* which inherited first this land, and after his name was called *Britain*"] King *Henry* the Seventh is lineally descended by Issue-Male, saving one Woman, and is Son to *Brute* in five score Degrees.[26]

Arthur is not mentioned in the report, but it does not follow that his prime significance is in the least minimized. When looked upon in historical perspective, the Trojan and the Arthurian legend cannot be entirely disassociated in their effect on Tudor England. Geoffrey of Monmouth in virtually creating the one legend had linked it fast as steel to the other (Chaucer thought of "English Gaufride" as "besy for to bere up Troye"), and Arthur became the most distinguished Trojan in the English pantheon, or, for that matter, in the whole of northwestern Europe.[27] As a restorer of the glory that was Brutus, Arthur thus came to be joined continuously with Brutus in the devotion of Tudor primitivism. Nevertheless, "it was Arthur rather than Brut whom Geoffrey centralised as the hero of his epos and it was Arthur that (in more senses than one) the public would not willingly let die." [28] As a popular deliverer, Arthur shared honors to a lesser degree with Cadwalader,[29] for the loyal Welsh recognized Henry's cognizance, the Red Dragon, identified in Rouge Dragon of the College of Arms,[30] primarily as the cognizance of Uther Pendragon and Arthur.[31]

Henry's popularity increased with the birth of the Prince of Wales, whom, according to Francis Bacon, "the King (in honour of the *Brittish-Race*, of which himselfe was) named ARTHUR, according to the Name of that ancient worthy King of the *Britaines*; in whose Acts there is truth enough to make him Famous, besides that which is Fabulous." [32] The more nearly contemporary testimony of John Twyne bears a similar import:

Si quidèm vnquàm fuit aùt futurus est princeps in *Britannia,* in quo, (insit modò fides vaticinijs,) *Arthuri* virtutes rediuiuas relucescere oportebat, hic certè fuit: in quo generis antiquę nobilitas, & virtutis egregię laus vero Arthuro dignę, verè emicuerunt. Cuius rei vt apertius de se specimen aederet, quem primùm ex tantis nuptijs suscepit filium, *Arthurum* dici voluit: vt ad antiqui *Arthuri* gloriam quam à patre acceperat, ne nomen quidèm ipsum in filio desideraretur. [33]

Arthur Tudor was born on September 19, 1486, in Winchester Castle, where the traditional Round Table was preserved. [34] On November 29, 1489, he was created Prince of Wales, the first of the Tudors to receive the title. This event was celebrated by John Skelton in *Prince Arturis Creacyoun,* [35] and by Bernard André in *De Arturi principis creatione.* The blind André, royal poet laureate and tutor of the Prince, calls him "Arturus secundus," and praises his princely qualities:

Suavissimas flagrantissimasque rosas, purpuream videlicet ac niveam Arturus ipse uno eodemque stipite pululans tanta prosperitate secundavit ut omnium retro principum reliquorum famam ejus inclyta virtus, si non exsuperaverit, aequav[er]it certe.

In verses in honor of Prince Arthur's birth André writes:

Regius ecce puer Arturus surgit Olympo
Missus ab aethereo, nostri spes altera regni.[36]

And in the infant Prince of Wales he sees the
return of Arthur:

Haec est illa dies qua Arturi saecula magni
Effigiem pueri sub imagine cernere claram
Nostra queant.[37]

Giovanni de' Giglis, papal collector in England and
Bishop of Worcester in 1497, also sees the return
of Arthur in the Tudor prince:

Hic est quē veteres uidere uates
Venturū angligenis piū patronū
Arturus patrie pater decusq̦
Promissus populis uidendus atq̦
Post tot secula restitutus olim
Henrici soboles bonj parentis
Regis.[38]

In an epigram on the birth of Prince Arthur, Giglis
is more enthusiastic:

Quicūq̦ arturū vates predixerat olim
    Venturū reducem maximus ille fuit
Consilijs superū iamiā cognoscere fas est
    Affuit en dictis prestitit ipse fidem
Arturi rediere bonj nō nomina tantū
    Credite / Sed redeūt inclita facta uiri
Nunc sperare licet bruti tibi terra triūphos
    nūc tibi pax parta est nūc tibi certa quies
Ergo alacris trino tāto pro munere grates
    Anglia redde pias ac bona vota deo
Henrico et faueas potuit tibi surge princeps
    Non alio patrie de genitore pater.[39]

Pietro Carmeliano of Brescia, chaplain and Latin secretary to Henry, is even more lavish in praise of the Prince:

> Arthurus redijt per saecula tanta sepultus
>   Qui regum mundi prima Corona fuit.
> Ille licet corpus terris et membra dedisset:
>   Viuebat toto semper ī orbe tamen.
> Arthurum quisquis prędixerat esse secūdo
>   Venturum! uates maximus ille fuit.
> Arthuri nomen terras penetrauit ī omnes
>   Perpetuum faciunt fortia facta uirum
> Aurea iam redeūt cum prīncipe Sęcula tāto
>   Quęq3 diu Latuit/ iam dea uirgo redit
> Bellica iam tandem redijt cū prīcipe uirtus
>   Antiqūq3 decus anglia pulchra tuum.
> Vt primum arthurus iuueniles sumpserit ānos
>   Atq3 humeris poterit arma tenere suis!
> Sub iuga uicinos hostes: multosq́3 remotos
>   Mittet: et imperium proferet ille suū.
> Gesta patris uincet: proauos supabit et omnes:
>   Arthuri et ueteris gloria cedet ei.
> Indue Purpureas pro nato prīcipe uestes
>   Anglia: cesset opus: sit tibi festa dies.[40]

On October 17, 1498, Prince Arthur visited Coventry: "aȝenst whose coming was þe sponstrete ȝate garnysshed with the ix worthys and Kyng Arthur," who made the speech of welcome: "And this Balet was song at þe Crosse, Vivat le prynce Arthúr." [41] At the Prince's marriage with Catherine of Aragon on November 14, 1501, Bacon assures us, "King ARTHUR, the *Britton*, and the descent of the *Ladie* KATHERINE from the House of

LANCASTER, was in no wise forgotten." [42] Shortly
after the marriage the "Preins" and his bride were
sent to the borders of Wales to keep court at Ludlow Castle, and on this wise more favor was curried
with the Welsh. André states unreservedly that
over the "Britones," or "Wallenses," "Arturus
secundus, antenominati regis primogenitus princeps, cum haec scriberem dominabatur." [43] Only
the unfortunate death of Prince Arthur at Ludlow
on April 2, 1502, prevented his becoming King
Arthur indeed, and there is an interesting possi-
bility that he would have succeeded to the throne
of England as Arthur II. In Worcester Cathedral,
where the Prince was buried, there was erected in
1504 the "Chantry of Prince Arthur."

On August 8, 1503, at the marriage of Princess
Margaret to James IV of Scotland — a marriage
which aimed at the union of the Lion and the Uni-
corn [44] — "old King *Arthur* with his Knights of the
Round-Table were . . . brought upon the Lists." [45]
The son of this marriage, James V, the father of
Mary Queen of Scots, named a son Arthur: "Ar-
thurus Iacobi v filius. obiit in puerili aetate." [46]
The father of Tudor diplomacy was not a king for
nothing.

Although we have no evidence that Henry VIII
took official interest in his Welsh genealogy, nevertheless he continued the Tudor interest in Arthur:

"By cause his elder brother being named Arthure, he him selfe a most christian King for all heroicall vertues commendable, the rather seemed to fauour and further the aduancement of the fame of his most renoumed auncestor this same our ancient Arthure and the knightly traine of his rounde table." [47] After the death of Arthur Tudor, Henry, "frater eius nobilissimus," as Duke of York, was created Prince of Wales on February 18, 1503. His descent from the princes of Wales was worked out by Thomas Gardiner, a monk of Westminster: the pedigree begins with Cadwalader, and the "Gudly Owen of Wales" appears in the line. [48] Henry clearly realized the power of Arthurian association in the mind of the people, for on December 4, 1531, he had young Rhys ap Griffith, the grandson of Rhys ap Thomas, beheaded "for calling himself FitzUrien in commemoration of his ancestor Urien, the companion of Arthur and Lancelot." Henry "imagined that by adopting the word 'Fitz,' the boy was laying a claim to the sovereignty of Britain." [49] It was during Henry's reign, in 1536, that by an act of Parliament Wales was united to England.

In 1517 the Round Table in the Great Hall at Winchester was repaired, [50] and apparently before that time it was decorated in the Tudor white and green and with the Tudor Double Rose. In

June, 1520, the Nine Worthies appeared before
Henry and Francis I on the Field of the Cloth of
Gold near Calais:

Charlemaine, Arthur, & Godfry de Bulloigne . . .
were apparelled in long vestures of calendred cloth of
gold and purple clothe of gold broched together, with
whoddes and cappes of the same, visers & buskyns of
grene damaske.[51]

According to a French observer, presumably on
another day, over a "porte" there were three kings,

> dont celluy du meillieu estant vng peu plus
> hault tenant son sceptre royal en sa main dit
> en cestre maniere.
>
> Moy Artus roy chef de la table ronde
> Principal chef de tous cueurs vallereux
> Vueil receuoir de volunte parfonde
> Tous nobles cueurs par effect vertueux
> Princes puissans preux et audacieux
> Aymans honneur soubz vostre seigneurie
> Suyuez mes faitz et ma cheuallerie.[52]

Later in July, when Henry prepared to entertain
the young Emperor Charles V in a gorgeous ban-
queting house, over a "portail" were placed the
statues of three kings:

Celle qui estoit au miellieu estoit . . . roy artus quí
tenoit vne table ronde a tous bons cheualiers et droic-
turiers a soustenir et deffendre tout le monde pourtāt
en ses armes dazur trois courōnes dor et en vng aulire
escu desoubz luy deux espees en camp dazur tenues de
deux mains ētrelacies de vne diuise. Cui adhereor pre
me est . . . cest a dire deuāt & cely a q̄ ie adhere.[53]

The device "has been understood to read 'He whom I cleave to is before me,' a motto which was intended to represent Henry's reverence for his Tudor ancestor."[54] On June 6, 1522, when Charles was again Henry's guest, in London,

att the Condytt in Cornhyll dyd stande a pageant off a goodly Castell well and rychely garnysshede and arayde where satte the ryght noble and victorious emprowr Kynge Arthur w[t] a crowne imperiall in complett harnes and a swerde in hys hande w[t] the rounde table before hyme.[55]

Or, according to Edward Hall,

betwene . . . two towers was a palice, vnder a rich clothe of estate sat kyng Arthur at a rounde table & was serued with x. kynges, Dukes and erles all bearyng Targettes of their armes, and when the Emperor and the kyng were commyng thither a Poet sayd.

> Laudat magnanimos vrbs inclita Roma Catones
>   Cantant Hannibalem punica regna suum
> Gentis erat Solime rex ingens gloria Dauid.
>   Gentis Alexander gloria prima sue.
> Illustrat fortes Arthuri fama Britannos
>   Illustras gentem Cesar & ipse tuam
> Cui deus imperium victo precor hoste secundet
>   Regnet vt in terris pacis amica quies.[56]

At Winchester on June 22 the Round Table was one of the objects of chivalry displayed.[57]

Under the steady growth of centralization of power and with the separation of the English church from papal authority, the spirit of nationalism grew intenser still. In his Act of Supremacy in 1534 Henry alleged as a ground for separation that Britain had once been an empire. Previously he had given official recognition to the antiquarian movement by appointing John Leland King's Antiquary. Leland took his post solemnly. In addition to his topographical and geographical writings, which circulated in manuscript during his lifetime, Leland's *Assertio inclytissimi Arturij Regis Britanniae* (1544),[58] dedicated to his king and directed against Polydore Vergil's *Anglicae Historiae Libri XXVI* (Basel, 1534),[59] constitutes the first chauvinistic defence of the authenticity of Arthur as portrayed by Geoffrey of Monmouth.[60] The fact that this defence fired anew the national zeal about the figure of Arthur and precipitated a "sixteenth century battle of the books"[61] which lasted well into the Stuart period justifies a notice of Polydore's remarks on Geoffrey:

There hathe appeared a writer in owre time which, to purge these defaultes of Brittains, feininge of them thinges to be laughed at, hathe extolled them aboove the noblenes of Romains and Macedonians, enhauncinge them with moste impudent lyeing. This man is cauled Geffray, surnamed Arthure, bie cause that oute of the olde lesings of Brittons, being somwhat augmented bie him, hee hathe recited manie things of this King Arthure, taking unto him bothe the coloure of Latin speeche and the honest pretext of an Historie: more over, taking in hande a greater enterprice, he hathe published the sowthesaiengs of one Merlin, as prophesies of most assuered and approved trewthe, allways addinge somwhat of his own while he translatede [62] them into Latine.[63]

Polydore writes further of Arthur:

Arthur, being noe doubte suche a mann as, if hee hadd lived longe, hee surelie woulde have restored the whole somme beeing allmoste loste to his Britons. As concerninge this noble prince, for the marvelus force of his boddie, and the invincible valiaunce of his minde, his posteritee hathe allmoste vaunted and divulged suche gestes, as in our memorie emonge the Italiens ar commonlie noysed of Roland, the nephew of Charles the Great bie his sister, allbeit hee perished in the floure of his yowthe; for the common people is at this presence soe affectioned, that with woonderus admiration they extol Arthure unto the heavens.[64]

There is, to be sure, little of a condemnatory nature in Polydore's account [65] — the chronicler Fabyan says as much, and Giraldus Cambrensis had flaunted his skepticism almost in Geoffrey's own face — but the fact that Polydore was an Italian, a foreigner, even though a naturalized Englishman, was enough to cause Leland to take up the cudgels in favor of "noster Arturius Britanniae." A typical line of Leland's argument in the *Assertio* is revealed by his comment on Polydore's using Gildas' failure to mention Arthur as evidence of Arthur's never having lived: "Hoccine est Italicum acu-

men?" [66] Yet it is the sincerity of Leland's national prejudice that arrests our attention:

Nam ego probè noui, quàm mihi sit curta domi
supellex.[67]

In a word, Leland was greatly impressed by the
"proofs" of Arthur's historicity which distorted
the judgment of Caxton:

Also galfrydus in his brutysshe book recounteth his
lyf/ and in dyuers places of England/ many remem-
braunces ben yet of hym and shall remayne perpetuelly/
and also of his knyghtes/ Fyrst in the abbey of west-
mestre at saynt Edwardes shryne remayneth the prynte
of his seal in reed Waxe closed in beryll/ In whych is
wryton Patricius Arthurus/ Britannie/ Gallie/ Ger-
manie/ dacie/ Imperator/ Item in the castel of douer ye
may see Gauwayns skulle/ & Cradoks mantle. At wynchester the rounde table/ in other places Launcelottes
swerde and many other thynges/ Thenne al these
thynges consydered there can no man resonably gayn-
saye but there was a kyng of thys lande named Arthur/[68]

For Leland in the *Assertio* upholds the fame of
Arthur in opposition as well to William of Newburgh, Hector Boece, and others unnamed —

non procul à regno est, quale meritò vel Alexandrino
praeferam.[69]

It is not surprising, therefore, that he saw in Henry
VIII both *Arturius alter* [70] and *Arturius rediuiuus*:

Optima spes rerum maestos solata Britānos
Sorte reuicturum promisit, & omine laeto

Arturum, obscuro lucem qui redderet orbi.
Tempus adest.   Victor prodit rediuiuus in auras,
Festa triumphali redimitus tempora lauro.
Hoc quoque ueridici uates cecinêre futurum.
Martia caeruleos repetit sic palma Britannos.[71]

In *A cōmendacion of welshmen* (1546),[72] Arthur
Kelton sings the glory of all the Welsh, and lavishes
praise upon Henry VII, Henry VIII, and Prince
Edward.   Kelton's halting measures may be con-
doned when he strives

> Some payne to take
> For desires sake
> And herty assuraunce
> With yncke and penne
> The gentill Walshmenne
> Their fame to aduaunce.

From "noble Troy" came the "whole procrea-
cion," [73]

> Of whose succession
> By conputacion
> Of ther parentage
> Perceaue maye ye
> That welshmen be
> Of the same stocke & lynage[74]

"Brutus Albinus" is the

> Most noble brute
> The seede, the frute
> The name and language
> The playne discent
> The norishement
> Of the welshmens linage [75]

and

A treatile.

Oue and delire
Dooeth me require
So effectually
J can no lelle
Of gentilnelle
But graunt it willyngly.

⁊Some payne to take
For delires lake
And herty alluraunce
With yncke and penne
The gentill Walchmenne
Their fame to aduaunce.

⁊As lhall inlewe
Matter tull trewe
By ltoris euiedent
Of auctours olde
Bothe wꝛite and tolde
Famous and excellent

⁊Trultyng in this
No man thereis
a.iii.   My

Signature a.iii., the First Surviving Page
of Arthur Kelton's *Commendacion of
welshmen*, 1546. (Henry E. Huntington
Library)

Thus maye ye se
That welshmen be
Of the blood imperiall
Of nature fre
Cosyns in degre
To the goddes immortall [76]

.   .   .   .   .

Likewyse syth Brute
Did institute
Cambre fyrst into wales
Ther to remayne
In roughe and playne
Among moūtaynes & vales

Yet vnto this daye
Perceyue ye maye
Thesame stocke & lynage [77]

Among the "Kinges of renowne" Kelton places
Arthur:

The cheiffe victour
Prouid at all assayes [78]

.   .   .   .   .

Twelue battelles stronge
He had them amonge
Like a famous champion
By strength imperiall
He was victore of all
Brought them to subiection

Auctores do expresse
Bering full wyttnesse
Of his magnificence
With his owne hand
Their might to withstande
Of knightly excellence [79]

Cadwalader, the "famose worthy king," is

> The last of dyscent
> A Prince Excellent
> Ouer the Britones raynyng[80]

From Cadwalader's line in "the fourth genera-cyon" [81] sprang Henry VII:

> The Last famose king
> Ouer vs rainyng
> Namid the seuynth henry
> Was euen the same
> Whose princely name
> Was had in suche memory
>
> Predestinate
> And animate
> By heuenly influence
> For to fulfyll
> The deuine will
> Of the highe magnyficence [82]

The printed marginal commentary is significant:

Henry y̆ vii of Cadwaladers line rightfull kyng of Britayne called Englond [83]

Henry VIII is the

> Most noble Henry
> Called theight of that name
> Whose gyftes naturall
> Aboue princes all
> Bereth awaye the fame [84]

The marginal commentary is again significant:

Henry y̆ viii. sonne of Henry y̆ vii kyng of England, I whom is fulfillid the mistery of Cadwaladers transla-tion [85]

After Henry VIII comes

> Yong Prince Edwarde
> To supply his regalle place [86]

We need not inquire whether such enthusiasts as Leland and Kelton are correct in their conclusions: it is the very enthusiasm that matters. The England of the Tudors is beginning to reap the inheritance of the Britain of Brutus and Arthur and Cadwalader.

In 1547 Kelton dedicated a more elaborate work to the young King Edward VI as "Kynge of Englande, Fraunce and Irelande, and in yearthe the supreme heade of the Churche of Englande and Irelande": "A Chronycle with a Genealogie declaryng that the Brittons and Welshemen are lineallye dyscended from Brute. Newly and very wittely compyled in Meter." In this metrical chronicle Kelton takes up Leland's attack on Polydore Vergil:

> We speake to you, Master *Polidorus*
> Whose ingratitude, we greatly complain
> Ye go aboute, to rase out the floures
> Of our parentes, as thynges in vain
> And yet of truthe, ye cannot refrain
> But generally, vs to accuse
> No indifferency, herin ye vse.
>
> We Welshemen saie for our defence
> That ye Romayns, surmountyng in pride
> With your Imperiall magnificence

> Supposyng therby, the heuens to deuide
> Came long after, our noble tribe
> So that we maie, write of your estate
> Not ye of vs, ye came all to late.[87]

Arthur is

> Noble Arthur the famous Brute
> Of the same line, and true succession [88]

Kelton queries:

> Who wer more worthy, then wer these three
> Hercules, Hector, and Arthur the kyng
> For their princely Magnanimitee
> Was neuer none, to them resemblyng
> In bodely strength, all other surmountyng
> Lions, Dragons, monsterous and wild
> By manly cōstraint, made them tame & milde[89]

Let the Romans have their Cæsar, the Trojans their Hector, the Persians their Alexander, the Greeks their Achilles, and the Carthaginians their Hannibal, but

> we Arthur most worthyest of all
> Ought to remember, in our fantasy
> Passyng all other, in deedes marciall
> Like Mars him selfe, shinyng in glory
> In his triumphes, conquest and victory
> As the story of him dothe recounte
> All other kinges in his tyme dyd surmount.[90]

And "our kyng" Edward VI surpasses the Worthies of all other countries. In a concluding "Genealogy of the Brutes" Edward is in direct line from Brutus and "Arthur the gret."

In his *Illustrium Maioris Britanniae Scriptorum, hoc est, Angliae, Cambriae, ac Scotiae Summariū* (1548), John Bale continues the defence of "Galfridus Arthurius" against Polydore Vergil. He advances a line of argument that is iterated and reiterated throughout the century: "Interpres autē Galfridus erat, non fictor historie." [91] Edward VI's reign also heard sounded the summons for the publication of England's antiquities. In 1549 Bale wrote as follows in the preface to his edition of *The laboryouse Iourney & serche of Iohan Leylande, for Englandes Antiquitees*:

As ye fynde a notable Antyquyte, suche as are the hystoryes of Gildas & Nēnius amonge the Brytaynes, Stephanides & Asserius amōg the Englyshe Barons, lete them anon be imprented, & so brynge them into a nombre of coppyes, both to their and your owne perpetuall fame. [92]

To the list of skeptics as to the ancient British history, Bale adds Boccaccio:

For so lytle estemynge our true Antiquytees, the proude Italyanes haue alwayes holdē vs for a Barbarouse nacyon. Loke Iohan Boccatius in hys sixt boke *de genealogia Deorum, Cap.* lvij. where as he treateth of *Syluius posthumus* and of our Brute, besydes their hystoryans. [93]

In 1550 John Coke, "clarke of the kynges recognysaunce," brought out *The Debate betwene the*

Heraldes of Englande and Fraunce, which he modelled on *Le Débat des Hérauts* attributed to Charles d'Orléans. The curious work is interesting, among other things, for its blind patriotism and its exaggeration of England's greatness at the expense of France. The picture of an imperialistic Arthur of England points forward to important developments during the Elizabethan age:

Arthur kyng of Englande, conquered Irlande, Goteland, Denmarke, Fryselande, Norway, Iselande, Grenelande, Orkeney, Lecto, Fraunce, Almayne, Nauerne, Espayne, Portȳgale, Aragon, Prouence, Sauoy, Burgoyne, Flaunders, Brabant, Henalde, Holande, Zelande, Geldres, and all Italy, . . . he kylled Lucius the Consul in battayle, and with all glory and victory at the Capitole in the sea Imperial in Rome was crowned Emperoure. . . . This myghty cōquerour for this valiaūces most glorious and marcial actes is the fyrst & chyefe of the nyne worthies beyng christened and was the most lyberall, coragious, worthiest, famous and redoubted prynce of the earth.[94]

Mary I was reckoned as a direct descendant of "Goodly" Owen Tudor and Catherine,[95] and at the reception of Philip II of Spain in London in 1554, out of compliment to her, the Nine Worthies appeared with Henry VIII and Edward VI in the list, and with Mary herself as a Woman Worthy:

From London Bridge they passed to the Conduit in Gracious streete whiche was finely painted, and among other thinges, the .ix. worthyes, whereof Kyng Henry the eyght was one. He was painted in harnesse hauyng in one hand a sworde, and in the other hand a booke, whereupon was written *Verbum Dei*, deliueryng the same booke (as it were) to hys sonne K. Edward, who was Painted in a corner by hym.

But hereupon was no small matter made, for the Byshop of Winchester Lord Chauncellor, sent for the Painter and not onely called hym knaue for paintyng a booke in kyng Henries hand and specially for writing thereupon *Verbum Dei*, but also rancke Traytour and Villayne, saying to him that hee should rather haue put the booke into the Quenes hand (who was also paynted there) for that she had reformed the church and religion, with other thinges, according to the pure and sincere word of God in deede. . . . So the Paynter departed, but fearyng lest he shoulde leaue some parte eyther of the booke, or of *Verbum Dei* in kyng Henries hand: hee wyped away a peece of hys fingers withall.[96]

In a parliamentary oration of December in the same year Cardinal Reginald Pole was more careful than the painter, and declared that England first of all islands received the faith of Christ:

For the Britaines beyng fyrst inhabitauntes of this Realme (notwithstandyng the subiectiō of the Emperours and Heathen Princes) dyd receyue Christes fayth from the Apostolicke Sea vniuersally, and not in partes as other Countreyes nor by one and one, as Clockes encrease theyr houres by distinction of tymes, but altogether at once, as it were in a moment.[97]

Julian del Castillo, who began chronicling in 1579, tells an interesting story of the marriage of his king to Mary at Winchester on July 25, suggesting, it seems, that the Round Table was redecorated for the occasion:

En el de 1554. . . . el Catolico Rey dō Filipe II. . . . se casò en Inglaterra en Hunchristre, donde està la tabla redonda de los veinte y quatro Caualleros, que instituyò y ordenò el Rey Artus de Inglaterra, como se ha dicho: la quel mesa es de veinte y quatro girones, lo ancho dellos a la parte de fuera, y las puntas adentro, que van a dar todas a la Rosa de Inglaterra, que està en medio; y el Rey Artus pintado con vna espada en la mano, y en lo ancho de los girones hàzia fuera està escritos los nombres de los Caualleros della; y los girones son blancos, y verdes: y es fama comun, que el Rey Artus està encantado en aquella tierra en figura de cueruo; y ay entre ellos grandes penas contra el que matare cueruo; y que ha de boluer a reynar: y cierto dizen, que fu Magestad del Rey don Filipe II. jurò, que si el Rey Artus viniesse en algun tiēpo, le dexaria el Reyno.[98]

Ticknor concludes that these words imply "at least in Castillo himself, and probably in many of his readers, a full faith in the stories of Arthur and his Round Table." [99]

In Mary's reign, then, the fire of Arthurian interest did not burn in indirect proportion to the leaping flames of the human bonfires of West Smithfield. Mary, like her grandfather, her father, and her brother, had Welsh blood in her veins, and she received the compliment of "Princesse of Wales." [100]

CHAPTER III

The Reign of Elizabeth

Polydor and *Lel.* contend for *Arthur* withe Tothe and Nayle.
WILLIAM LAMBARD, *Dictionarium Angliae Topographicum & Historicum, ca.* 1577.

And she that sits in reagall Throne,
With Scepter, Sword, and Crowne.

(Who came from *Arthurs* rase and lyne).
THOMAS CHURCHYARD,
The Worthines of Wales, 1587.

THE interim of Mary I was too short-lived to be a setback to Tudor popularity, and on November 17, 1558 — when Spenser was a lad of six or more in East Smithfield — with the accession of Elizabeth, the great-great-granddaughter of Owen Tudor and herself the "beauteous Queene of second Troy," [1] the spirit of nationalism waxed full-blown and the tide of Arthurian enthusiasm in England reached its flood. On at least one occasion during the reign of Elizabeth the pedigree of the Penmynydd Tudor family is known to have been examined and recorded officially. Item 7 of Document 2093 of the Wynn of Gwydir Papers, which contains memoranda by Sir Owen Wynn of business to be transacted in London, presumably in 1655, reads in part as follows:

A Commission or writte (of diem clausit extremum)
yssued foorthe out of the Courte of Wards about 4°
Elizabeth: to find out what children Owen Tudyr esq. of
the bodie to prynce Arthur had.

To learne out from some clr̄es of the Courte of Wards
office wheere to find the retorne of that writt. or . . . . . .
and he shall have a gratuytie for his paynes findinge it
out.[2]

The numerous genealogies in manuscript which
place Elizabeth in the line from Arthur, Cadwalader, Owen Tudor, and Henry VII, show that
Elizabeth, "the last that remaineth aliue of that
lyne," [3] was considered by her subjects before the
date of *The Faerie Queene* as "the right inheritrice
of the Principalitie of *Wales*" and as a continuator
of the Welsh faery blood.[4] According to John
Selden, the Elizabethans had all faith in the prophecy which "foretold of a reuerting of the crowne,
after the *Britons*, *Saxons*, and *Normans* to the first
againe, which in *Hen. VII.* sonne [*i. e.*, grandson]
to *Owen Tyddour*, hath beene obserued, as fulfilled." [5] Lodowick Lloyd's broadside, *A Dittie to
the tune of Welshe Sydānen, made to the Queenes maj.'
Eliz.*, which was licensed on August 13, 1579, the
year of *The Shepheardes Calender*, refers to Elizabeth as Sidanen "from Cambers soile." [6] In *The
Blessednes of Brytaine* (1587), Maurice Kyffin calls
his Queen "her maiestie Princesse of Wales." [7]
Thomas Churchyard in *The Worthines of Wales*

(1587) — which was dedicated to Elizabeth, "a comfort to Wales, a glorie to England"—addresses her thus: "Gracious Lady, vnder your Princely fauour I haue vndertaken to set foorth a worke in the honour of Wales, where your highnes auncestours tooke name." [8] Later, in the midst of the medley of prose and verse, he praises her as "a Quéene of that race, who is descended of so noble a progenie,"

> she that sits in reagall Throne,
> With Scepter, Sword, and Crowne.

> (Who came from *Arthurs* rase and lyne).[9]

The union of the Red Dragon of Cadwalader (which was as significant in the Tudor coat of arms as the Royal Lion or the Beaufort Greyhound or the Dun Cow or the Double Rose of Lancaster and York) with the dragon of Uther Pendragon and Arthur was recognized by the Elizabethans, for Sir James Ley observes that "this dragon, or not much unlike, is one of the regal supporters at this present," [10] and he quotes from Geoffrey of Monmouth and further from "Matthew of Westminster" for proof of his assertion: "Vnde vsque hodie mos inoleuit regibus terrae huius, quod pro vexillo Draconem in bellicis expeditionibus ante se statuerint deferendum per Regem." [11]

The very scandal of Elizabeth's courting days, that cost many an Elizabethan a pair of eager ears

— the scandal that rumored the Queen to be the mistress of Robert Dudley, Earl of Leicester, and even to be the mother of a child by him — points toward her association with Arthur. Leicester himself at his entrance to Donhage on December 27, 1585, was honored by a comparison with "Arthur of Britaine," [12] and one B.C., an English spy on the preparation of the Armada, writes as follows from Madrid on May 28, 1588:

About xvj monthes agone was taken a Youthe entringe Spaine owte of France, about Fontarabie, who hathe gyven owte his person to be begotten betwene our Quene and the Erle of Leycester; borne att Hampton courte, and furthwith by the elder Assheley delyvered into the handes of one Southorne the servant to Mrs. Assheley, with charge upon payne of deathe that the sayde Southorne shoulde not revele the matter, but bringe ytt upp; who brought the babe to a myllers wyfe of Mowlsey to gyve ytt sucke, and afterwards the said Southorne goynge into his countrey whiche was Wurcester or Shropshier, caried with hym the chylde, and there brought ytt up in learnynge and qualyties. In the ende, discoveringe unto this youthe the whole secrete, he tooke a flyght over sees, where many yeres he hathe remayned untill his commynge hyther. His name is Arthure, and of xxvij yeres of age, or there about. This forsoothe ys his sayenge, and takethe upon hym lyke to the man he pretendethe to be; wherupon he wanteth no kepers, and is very solemply warded and served, with an expence to this Kinge of vj crownes a daye.[13]

In view of Arthur's inclusion among the Nine Worthies,[14] it is of interest that Elizabeth was com-

plimented by being placed among the Nine
Women Worthies, who sprang up by happy parallel
to the Nine Muses and to the Nine Worthies themselves.[15] Elizabeth occupied a rôle in English history like that of her preceding sister English
Worthies: Boadicea, or "*Bunduica*, that valiant
manlike dame";[16] Ethelfleda, daughter of Alfred;
Matilda, or "Maud," who "neuer desisted from
the fielde, till that the vsurped *Stephen* of Bloys,
had condiscended to her sons right";[17] Margaret,
wife of Henry VI, who led the Lancastrians against
Edward IV; Mary I, who figured as a Worthy in a
pageant in honor of her marriage with Philip II of
Spain. In John Ferne's *Blazon of Gentrie* (1586), in
which a list of the Nine Women Worthies appears,
England's Welsh queen is "*Elizabeth* our *Hester*,
Delbora, and *Iudith*." [18] In Henry Lyte's *Light of
Britayne* (1588), she is the

M*OST* dread soueraigne Ladie Elizabeth, by the grace of
God: The Phœnix of the worlde: The Angell of Englande:
The bright Britona of Britayne: euen Britomartis Presi-
dent of Britaine.[19]

For the motivation of *The Faerie Queene*, such in-
sistencies on the martial virtue of Elizabeth, or on
what Thomas Heywood calls her "masculine magnanimity," [20] share importance with the repeated
stress on her Welsh descent.

Elizabeth's own concern about her Welsh de-

scent and her sovereign right to the British empire
is amply shown by her approval of Doctor John
Dee's report on

Her Majesties Title Royall, to many forrain Countries, kingdomes, and provinces, by good testimony and
sufficient proofe recorded: and in 12 Velam skins of
Parchment, faire written: for her Majesties use: and at
her Majesties commandement — Anno 1578.[21]

An entry in Dee's diary for 1580 tells of his meeting
with the Queen:

Oct. 3rd, on Munday, at 11 of the clok before none, I
delivered my two rolls of the Quene's Majesties title
unto herself in the garden at Richemond, who appointed
after dynner to heare furder of the matter. Therfore
betwene one and two afternone, I was sent for into her
highnes Pryvy Chamber, where the Lord Threasurer
allso was, who, having the matter slightly then in con-
sultation, did seme to dowt much that I had or could
make the argument probable for her highnes' title so as
I pretended.[22]

Though Elizabeth herself was enthusiastic over the
document prepared "at her Majesties commandement," Lord Burghley, as we should expect, was at
first skeptical; but a few days later, on October 10,

the Quene's Majestie . . . told me that the Lord Threas-
orer had gretly commended my doings for her title,
which he had to examyn, which title in two rolls he had
browght home two howrs before.[23]

Burghley's own abstract of "M Dees book"[24] begins with the statement "That Arthur kyng of

Britā was y̆ᵉ Conqr̄ōr of these Contryes." ²⁵ From
the list of Arthur's conquests which follows and
from the marginal commentary ("in legibus boni
Regis Edwardi quas wˢ Cōquiſtr· Confirmavit"),²⁶
it appears that Dee's report was based on a document printed in William Lambard's *APXAIO-
NOMIA, siue de priscis anglorum legibus libri*
(1568): "De iure & appendicijs coronae regni Brytanniae," ²⁷ which Lambard quotes as among the
laws of Edward the Confessor and which has the
familiar imperialistic ring of Geoffrey of Monmouth's *Historia* and Alanus de Insulis' commentary on the *Prophecies of Merlin*.²⁸ On the warrant
of the laws of Edward the Confessor, Lambard also
attributes to Arthur the old custom of "folcmote,"
the swearing of fealty to the king in the presence
of the king's bishop:

> Hanc legem inuenit Arthurus, qui quondā fuit in-
> clytissimus rex Brytonum, & ita consolidauit, & con-
> faederauerit regnum Brytanniae vniuersum semper in ²⁹
> vnum. Huius legis authoritate expulit Arthurus pre-
> dictus Saracenos, & inimicos a regno.³⁰

On the authority of a Christian Arthur's expulsion
of Saracens, and all enemies whatsoever to England, Elizabeth could without qualm consider herself supreme head of the Church of England, even
as Henry VIII had cited the fact that Britain had
once been independent of Rome as a ground for
separation.

But John Dee has left us matter more momentous, matter that brings us close to Spenser. In his autobiographical remains he repeatedly refers to the "IMPERIAL BRYTISH MONARCHIE" and the "BRYTISH QUEENE ELIZABETH," and in one of his few works published during his lifetime — *General and Rare Memorials pertayning to the Perfect Arte of Nauigation* (1577) — he had already broached the matter which led to his confirmation of the Queen's title to empire. This book, which Dee refers to in his diary as "my work of Imperium Brytanicum" [31] and which bears the running title of *The Brytish Monarchie*, was directed against those who "haue gone about, to ouerthrow, and confound, this blessed Brytish Monarchy." [32] It is in the main a plea on the basis of the power of "that Triumphant BRYTISH ARTHVR" [33] and of "that good King Edgar" [34] for a "Pety Nauy Royall" [35] to guard "this Incomparable Brytish Impire" and "the Royall Maiesty, and Imperiall Dignity of our Souerayn Lady Elizabeth, (within her own Sea Limits)." [36] Dee had also broached the matter of Elizabeth's imperial title to Elizabeth herself before the day on which he delivered the manuscript. An entry in his diary for November 28, 1577, reads as follows:

I spake with the Quene hora quinta; I spake with Mr. Secretary Walsingham. I declared to the Quene her title to Greenland, Estetiland and Friseland. [37]

A further entry, for 1578, brings Arthur himself into Dee's conversation and shows conclusively what Dee was about:

June 30th, I told Mr. Daniel Rogers, Mr. Hackluyt of the Middle Temple being by, that Kyng Arthur and King Maty [= Malgo] ... did conquier Gelindia, lately called Friseland, which he so noted presently in his written copy of Monumethensis, for he had no printed boke therof.[38]

Significance is at once attached to Gabriel Harvey's words in his letter to Spenser in May, 1580, in which he states that he has returned to Spenser "your *Faerie Queene*." Harvey includes some of his "Patcheries, and fragments" of reformed versifying, and cautions Spenser to show them to none save those "two Gentlemen" Sidney and Dyer, "vnlesse haply you have a special desire to imparte some parte hereof, to my good friend *M. Daniel Rogers*: whose curtesies are also registred in my Marble booke." [39] No light has yet been thrown on the degree of Spenser's acquaintanceship with the diplomatist and antiquary Daniel Rogers, the friend also of Sidney, Languet, and Camden.[40] As for Dee, one form of his writings was certainly known to Spenser, for, as a supposed letter to Spenser shows, Harvey knew that the poet would understand the reference to "the mysticall and supermetaphisicall philosophy of Doctor

Dee." [41] Dee, who has left record of one visit paid him by Sidney, Edward Dyer, and Robert Dudley, Earl of Leicester, in the same company,[42] is an ideal example of the historical primitivism of his age. Among the slight marginalia in his own manuscript copy of the *Historia*, he took care to gloss Geoffrey's "Aper . . . cornubiae" by "Rex Arthur," [43] and he kept the name of Arthur in the family by giving it to a son,[44] at whose christening Dyer stood as a godfather. The literary conversation in Spenser's circle after the poet's final graduation from Cambridge was not entirely devoted to experiments in classical metres.

In the case of the elder Hakluyt, who was in John Dee's presence with Daniel Rogers on June 30, 1578, when Dee was citing Geoffrey of Monmouth for the conquests of Arthur — Dee's audience with Elizabeth on November 28, 1577, should be kept in mind — such conversations as Dee sponsored bore ripe fruit. The younger Hakluyt begins *The Second Part of the principall Nauigations, Voyages and Discoueries of the English nation* (1589) with "*Certaine testimonies concerning king Arthur and his Conquests of* the North Regions, taken out of the historie of the Kings of England, written by *Galfridus Monumetensis*, and newly printed at Heidelberge, An. 1587." [45] Hakluyt also gives "A testimonie of the right and appendances of the crowne of the kingdome of Britaine," which is translated from Lambard's "De iure & appendicijs coronae regni Brytanniae" in his *APXAIONOMIA* (1568). The extracts which have been quoted from Dee's diary render necessary a selection from Hakluyt's translation:

Arthur which was sometimes the most renowmed king of the Britains, was a mightie, and valiant man, and a famous warrior. This kingdome was too litle for him, and his mind was not contented with it. He therefore valiantly subdued all *Scantia*, which is now called *Norway*, and all the Islands beyond *Norway*, to wit *Island* and *Greenland*, which are appertaining vnto *Norway*, *Sweueland, Ireland, Gotland, Denmarke, Semeland, Windland, Curland, Roe, Femeland, Wireland, Flanders, Cherilland, Lapland*, and all the other lands and Islands of the East sea euen vnto *Russia* (in which *Lapland* he placed the Easterly bounds of his Brittish Empire) and many other Islands beyond *Norway*, euen vnder the North pole, which are appendances of *Scantia*, now called *Norway*. These people were wild and sauage, and had not in them the loue of God nor of their neighbors, because all euill commeth from the North, yet there were among them certaine Christians liuing in secret. But king Arthur was an exceeding good Christian, and caused them to be baptized, and throughout all *Norway* to worship one God, and to receiue and keepe inuiolably for euer, faith in Christ onely. At that time all the noble men of *Norway* tooke wiues of the noble nation of the Britaines, whereupon the *Norses* say, that they are descended of the race and blood of this kingdome. The aforesayd king Arthur obteined also in those dayes of the Pope & court of Rome, that *Norway*

should be for euer annexed to the crown of Britaine for
the inlargement of this kingdome, and he called it the
chamber of Britaine. For this cause the *Norses* say,
that they ought to dwell with vs in this kingdome, to
wit, that they belong to the crowne of Britaine.[46]

About three centuries later, the very idea of such
claims for British empire, which the Hakluyts
and Dee evidently considered modest enough,
would have given imperial Disraeli pause and sent
Victoria to her bed. In Hakluyt's reference to
Geoffrey's "historie of the Kings of England,"
Arthur is claimed as an English king, and his conquests as related by Geoffrey are cited for the glory
of England and for the glory of the growing British
empire of Elizabeth. The primitivistic appeal is
little less enthusiastic than Alanus de Insulis' interpretation of a part of the *Prophecies of Merlin*:

Quò enim Arturi Britonis nomen fama volans non
pertulit & vulgavit: quousque Christianum pertingit
imperium? Quis, inquam Arturum Britonem nō lo-
quatur, cum penè notior habeatur, Asiaticis gentibus,
quàm Britannis; sicut nobis referunt Palmigeri nostri de
orientis partibus [47] redeuntes? Loquuntur illum orien-
tales, loquuntur occidui, toto terrarum orbe diuisi.
Loquitur illum Ægyptus Bosforus exclusa non tacet.
Cantat gesta ejus domina civitatum Roma, nec emulam
quōdam ejus Carthaginem, Arturi praelia latent.
Celebrat actus ejus Antiochia, Armenia, Palaestina.[48]

Welsh blood was loyal; the earlier Tudors had
already made up England's mind about Scotland;

but it was necessary to mention Arthur's conquest of Ireland, about which another word must be added. Edmund Campion, in fact, unlocks several words:

Thus had the Brittaines an elder right to the Realme of Ireland, then by the conquest of *Henry* the 2. vvhich title they never surceased to claime, & sometimes prevailed, as in the dayes of King *Arthur*, to vvhom the Irish Princes agnized their tribute and apparance, made at his Parliament in *urbe Legionū*, vvhich I take to be Westchester, called of old Carleon, as divers other citties vvere, vvherein the Romanes placed the legions.[49]

Irenæus in *A Veue of the Present State of Ireland* points out that "Ireland is by Diodorus Siculus, and by Strabo, called Brytannia, and a parte of Greate Bryttaine," and in the very next sentence he affirms: "Finally, it appeareth by good Record yet extante that King Arthure, and before him Gurgunt, had all that Iland in his alleagiaunce and subjection." [50] "Hibernia" appears, be it remembered, in Lord Burghley's summary of "M Dees Book." The Tudor claim of Arthurian descent was used not only "to support the Tudor claim to supremacy over the whole island, including Wales and Scotland," [51] but also to assert Tudor supremacy over Ireland — a supremacy which Arthur, Lord Grey of Wilton, with Spenser as a secretary, went over to enforce in 1580. Further implication of Irenæus' phrasing, "Greate Bryt-

taine," is shown by a comparison with the claims
of John Hardyng, who, after asserting that Arthur

> also gatte as chronicles haue vs lered
> Denmarke, Friselande, Gotelande, and Norwaie
> Iselande, Grenelande, thisle of Man & Orknaie,[52]

proclaims

> Arthure kyng of all y̆ great Britain
> And Emperoure [53] of Roome, by title of right.[54]

Hardyng was one of the most imperialistic of the
fifteenth-century Arthurian chroniclers; he was
popularized by Richard Grafton in the sixteenth
century [55] — he is even ranked as a poet by the
author of *The Arte of English Poesie* (1589); and
Elizabethans carried his idea of *the great* Britain
an Arthurian stride farther. The author of *The
First Book of the Preseruation of King Henry the
vij* (1599), whom some would have to be Gabriel
Harvey, calls Elizabeth "the magnipotent, the renowned princes of *Europ*, Emperes *Elizabeth*." [56]
The idea for the change of *great* Britain into *Great
Britain* was not an innovation on the part of the
House of Stuart.

The profound political significance of basing
on the conquests of Arthur of Britain England's
claims, not only for a united Great Britain including Ireland but also for an empire extending across
the seas, was enhanced by the very presence of a

Welsh Queen "who came from *Arthurs* rase and lyne." What had begun as substantially a vindication of the ancient Britons and their descendants in Tudor England had become within fifty odd years a unified passion "to bring home England to the English," [57] and Arthur of England was used in a way that makes the Angevin Anglicization of Arthur of Britain seem pale and sporadic. To the majority of the Elizabethans, Arthur of England was as real as Alfred, Cadwalader, or Henry VII. Calais lived on in Elizabeth's heart as it had died in Mary's, and Elizabeth, upheld by the English Lion and the Welsh Dragon, with the sword "IVSTITIA" lying athwart "VERBUM DEI," did not hesitate to assume the title "D. G. ANGLIÆ FRANCIÆ ET HIBERNIÆ REGINA." It may be contended that once Spenser set himself to glorify Elizabeth, it was inevitable that he should use the Arthurian legend, but the inevitability does not preclude the workings of the old law of cause and effect. The conversations of John Dee, Daniel Rogers, the elder Hakluyt, Lord Burghley, and Elizabeth herself help to explain the inevitability.

By the time of Spenser, therefore, the Arthurian right of Tudor sovereigns had been made a firm historical tradition, a tradition sanctioned by Elizabeth herself; and we should well expect that Spenser's ideas for the inclusion of Arthurian story in

The Faerie Queene became as much a part of him
during his formative period as his notions of classical mythology or Platonic love. Before the reign of
Elizabeth, indeed, the Arthurian legend in connection with the Tudors had enjoyed, as we have already observed, a little Renaissance all its own, and
the Arthurian right of Tudor sovereigns had
reached Spenser as a poetical tradition as well.
That obscure poets had seized upon the connection
— be the Welsh, the Latin, the English however
crude — points to the applicability of the theme,
and we need not question whether all the Tudors
sponsored the flattery so long as they proved to be
patrons silently pleased. Henry VII had his Glyn
Cothi. Arthur, Prince of Wales, had his André,
his Giglis, his Carmeliano. Henry VIII had his
Leland. Edward VI had his Kelton. Mary alone
was without her Arthurian bard. How likely, then,
in view of the increased nationalism of the Elizabethan age, that Elizabeth should inspire an Arthurian throat in her "nest of singing birds"! As
Professor M. Y. Hughes has pointed out, Pierre de
Ronsard wrote verses to her — *A Très-Haute et
Très-Illustre et Très-Vertueuse Elisabet Royne d'An-
gleterre* (1567) — in which he "sketched the Arthurian legend as the basis of English glory and
suggested an epic poem in honor of Arthur." [58] In
The Blessednes of Brytaine (1587), Maurice Kyffin
sounded a similar and a more pertinent note:

Ye Bryttish Poets, *Repeat in Royall Song,*
(*VVith waightie woords, vsde in King* Arthurs *daies*)
Th' Imperial Stock, *from whence your* Queene *hath sprong;*
Enstall in verse your Princesse *lasting prayes:*
  Pencerddiaid, *play on Auncient Harp, and Crowde:*
  Atceiniaid, *sing her prayses pearcing lowd.*[59]

Besides, many other ramifications of the legend
were to influence Spenser. The antiquarian movement was given a great impetus in 1572, when Matthew Parker, Archbishop of Canterbury, founded
the Elizabethan Society of Antiquaries, and the
old grudge against Polydore Vergil did not cease
with the words of Leland, Kelton, and Bale. As
Bishop Joseph Hall was quick to observe, the age of
Spenser was also the age of William Camden, and
the bishop's observation may be extended to include other diligent Elizabethan antiquaries of
whatever rank or file. Indeed, in his *Britannia*
(1586), Camden, who was never more than luke-
warm in his praise of Arthur, hinted at the timeli-
ness of a panegyric on the gallant defender of
Britain:

  Materies [Arthuri] proculdubiò doctissimi viri facul-
tate, & copia digna, qui tantum principem celebrando
propriam etiam ingenij laudem consequutus fuisset.
Fortissimus enim Britannici imperij propugnator hoc
solo nomine vel infoelicissimus videtur, quòd suę virtutis dignum pręconem non inuenerit.[60]

The reverence for all forms of England's glorious
past, in which Brutus and Arthur and other illus-

trious empire-builders shone out like beacons, added strength and spirit to the age which focussed round the defeat of the Spanish Armada in 1588; and back of the unified search for England's antiquities, back of the interest in the Arthurian legend, back of any other special influences which may have increased Spenser's own interest in the legend, is the motive of England's building for British empire.[61] It was an age in which loyalty to the crown was in itself patriotism.

For a number of years before 1569 Spenser was a pupil at Merchant Taylors School, of which Richard Mulcaster was headmaster. Professor Renwick, who has given the best discussion of the probable influence of Mulcaster on Spenser, writes as follows of Mulcaster's main educational work: "*The First Part of the Elementarie* was published in 1582, thirteen years after Spenser had gone to Cambridge, but Mulcaster, like every schoolmaster, was writing from long experience, and we may presume that Spenser was taught on somewhat these lines." [62] We may put in a like claim for the *Positions* (1581),[63] for it is in this work that Mulcaster makes a digression that is extremely significant for Spenser's future use of the Arthurian legend:

In the middest of so many earnest matters, I may be allowed to entermingle one, which hath a relice of mirth, for in praysing of *Archerie*, as a principall exercise, to the preseruing of health, how can I but prayse them, who professe it throughly, & maintaine it nobly, the friendly and franke fellowship of prince *Arthurs* knightes in and about the citie of *London*, which of late yeares haue so reuiued the exercise, so countenaūced the artificers, so enflamed emulation, as in thēselues for frindly meting, in workemen for good gayning, in companies for earnest comparing, it is almost growne to an orderly discipline, to cherishe louing society, to enrich labouring pouertie, to maintaine honest actiuity, which their so encouraging the vnder trauellours, and so encreasing the healthfull traine, if I had sacred to silence, would not my good freind in the citie maister *Hewgh Offly*, and the same my noble fellow in that order Syr *Launcelot*, at our next meeting, haue giuē me a sowre nodde, being the chiefe furtherer of the fact, which I commend, and the famosest knight, of the fellowship, which I am of? Nay would not euen prince *Arthur* himselfe maister *Thomas Smith*, and the whole table, of those wel known knights, & most actiue *Archers* haue layd in their chaleng against their fellow knight, if speaking of their pastime I should haue spared their names? whereunto I am easily led, bycause the exercise deseruing such praise, they that loue so praiseworthie a thing neither can of them selues, neither ought at my hand to be hudled vp in silence.[64]

Mulcaster speaks of "the fellowship, which I am of," of "those wel known knights," and of "our next meeting," with evident familiarity, and gives us reason to believe that the "fellowship of prince *Arthurs* knightes" was prominent in the social life of Elizabethan London. Such praise of Prince Arthur's Knights fits with the spirited patriotism which his *Elementarie* reveals was at the basis of his pedagogy: "*I loue* Rome, *but* London *better, I fauor* Italie, *but* England *more, I honor the* Latin, *but I worship the* English." [65]

Evidence of the existence in the reign of Henry VIII of a society of archers connected with Arthur is shown by one W. M. or W. H. in *A Remembrance of the Worthy Show and Shooting by the Duke of Shoreditch, and his Associates the Worshipful Citizens of London, upon Tuesday the 17th of September, 1583*: [66]

The Prince of famous memory, King Henry the Eighth, having read in the Chronicles of England, and seen in his own time how armies mixed with good Archers, have evermore so galled the enemy, that it hath been great cause of the victory; he being one day at Mile-end when Prince Arthur and his Knights were there shooting, did greatly commend the game, and allowed thereof, lauding them to their encouragement.

This noble King at another time keeping a princely court at Windsor, caused sundry matches to be made concerning shooting in the long-bow: and to which came many principal archers, who being in game and the up-shoot given, as all men thought, there was one Barlo yet remaining to shoot, being one of the king's guard; to whom the King very graciously said, win them all and thou shalt be Duke over all the archers. This Barlo drew his bow, and shooting won the best. Whereat the King greatly rejoiced, commending him for his good archery; and for that this Barlo did dwell in Shoreditch, the King named him Duke of Shoreditch.[67]

The immediate suggestion for a band of English archers under the leadership of a *Prince* Arthur, although archers are associated with Arthur in the romances, no doubt grew out of the association of archery with Arthur, Prince of Wales, who, according to report, "became so expert in the use of the long-bow, that a good archer was honored by being stiled *Prince Arthur*." [68] It was apparently the association with Arthur, Prince of Wales, together with the memory of Barlo's feat, that stimulated Elizabethan archery, "which, both by Prince Arthur and the Duke of Shoreditch, hath been greatly revived, and within these five years set forward at the great cost and charges of sundry chief citizens." [69]

Mulcaster's assertion that archery had been "of late yeares" revived is further verified by the licensing of several broadsides. The Duke of Shoreditch appears in a broadside licensed to Richard Jones on August 23, 1577.[70] Prince Arthur appears, according to the broadside licensed to Edward White, on August 19, 1579, the year of *The Shepheardes Calender*: "ye Renovacon of Archery. by. prince Arthure and his companions."[71] But that the Duke's men and Prince Arthur's Knights composed different organizations is attested to by a passage from *A Remembrance of the Worthy Show and Shooting*:

And this one thing is worthy of memory, that upon the day of Prince Arthur's shooting, which was five weeks before this show, the Duke . . . sent a buck of that season . . . to Prince Arthur, who was at his tent, which was at Mile-end green; he not only accepted the same, but also promised to have the Duke's courtesy in mind, if God lent him life.[72]

God lent him life, for on this occasion, September 17, 1583, Prince Arthur's Knights defended against the Duke's men a giant at the end of Houndsditch, "which since that giant lived belonged to Prince Arthur"; [73] and at the Duke's tent in Hogsden Fields a representative of Prince Arthur delivered a commendatory oration to the Duke.[74]

Of Mulcaster's own "fellowship," Prince Arthur's Knights, by far the most significant information is furnished by Richard Robinson.[75] In 1582 Robinson published "A Learned and True Assertion of the original, Life, Actes, and death of *the most Noble, Valiant, and Renoumed Prince Arthure*, King of great *Brittaine.* Who succeeding his father *Vther Pendragon*, and right *nobly gouerning this Land sixe and twentie yeares*, then dyed of a mortall wounde receyued in battell, *together with victory ouer his enemies.* . . . And was buried at *Glastenbury.* . . . An. 543." [76] This work,[77] a translation (with additions) of Leland's *Assertio inclytissimi Arturij Regis Britanniae* (1544), contains a triple dedication: to Arthur, Lord Grey of Wilton, "then

Infignia Illuftrium Patronorum, huius
opufculi felectorum.

D. ARTVRVS BARO
Gray, de VVilton.

D. HENRICVS SIDNEY, Illuftrifsimi (
dinis Garterij Miles, vnus Confiliario-
rum D. Reg. & in Principa-
tu Walliæ Præfid.

Magifter Thomas Smith D. Reginæ
Cuftumarius Principalis, in
Portu London.

Ecclef. 10.cap. Gloria Diuitum, Honoratorum, & Pauperum, eft
Timor Dei.

Richard Robinson's Translation of Leland's *Assertio*,
Signature A1ᵛ, Showing the Triple Dedication: to Arthur,
Lord Grey of Wilton, Sir Henry Sidney, and Thomas
Smith, Esquire, London's Prince Arthur. (British Mu-
seum C.38.d.6.)

To the Right Honorable Lord ARTHVRE
GRAY, *Baron of Wilton*, *Lord Deputie*
& Lieftenant Generall for the Queenes
Maieftie in Ireland:

To the Right Honorable Sir HENRY SIDNEY, Knight
of the Honorable Order of the Garter,& Prefident for
her Maieftie in the Marches of Wales:

To the Rightworfhipfull M. THOMAS SMITH, *Efquire,&*
Chiefe Cuftomer for her Maieftie in the Porte of London: & to the Wor-
fhipfull Societie of Archers, in London yearely celebrating the renowned memorie of the Magnificent Prince ARTHVRE & his
Knightly Order of the Round Table:

Grace, mercy, & Peace in the Lord Euerlaftinge.

AVING in mindefull memorie
(*Right Honourable, and Worfhipp-*
full) that mercifull couenaunt of
peace, by our omnipotent Crea-
tor towardes all flefh thus mani-
fefted(*I do fet my Raine Bowe in the* Gen. 9.
cloudes, & it fhall be as a tokē betwene
me & the earth) promifing hereby
neuer to deftroy the fame any
more by waters: how much ought mākind fpecially, en-
ioying by this peaceable pact, from Heauē, Earth, & the
Sea, abundance of benefittes: feare God in his holines,
loue one an other in righteoufneffe, and vfe thefe benefittes with thankfulneffe to the aduauncement of his
glory. For this Bowe, this Rainebowe I fay of his coue-
nānt, and pledge of his peace, left vnto vs frō the deluge
(as *Ariftotle* affirmeth) *Naturally appeareth by reflection* Arift meteor
or giuing backe of the light of the Sunne, from a cloude oppofite, or liber 3. Cap. 1,
againft the fame. So our heauēly God, the Father of light, Trac. 2.
and giuer of grace, departeth with the light of his
manifolde mercies vnto mankinde, from the oppofite
cloude of his difpleafure. Againe, this Bowe of his co-
A 2   uenant

Richard Robinson's Translation of Leland's *Assertio*,
Signature A2, Showing the Triple Dedication: to Arthur,
Lord Grey of Wilton, Sir Henry Sidney, and Thomas
Smith, Esquire, London's Prince Arthur. (British Mu-
seum C.38.d.6.)

her Maiestyes Leevetenant generall in Ireland who gave me here in London x s.," [78] whom Spenser joined as secretary in 1580; [79] to Sir Henry Sidney, the father of Philip; [80] and to Thomas Smith, [81] "*Esquire, &* Chiefe Customer for her Maiestie in the Porte of London," and "the Worshipfull Societie of Archers, in London yearely celebrating the renoumed memorie of the Magnificent Prince ARTHVRE & his Knightly Order of the Round Table." [82] In the dedicatory epistle Robinson gives further testimony to the existence of a Prince Arthur's Round Table of archers in the reign of Henry VIII:

By patent of his princely prerogatiue ordayned, graunted, and confirmed hee vnto this honorable Citie of London, free electiō of a Chieftaine and of Citizens representing the memory of that magnificent King Arthure, and the Knightes of the same order, which should for the mayntenance of shooting onely, meete together once a yeare, with solemne and friendly celebration therof. So much in his noble minde preuayled all prouident care of princely prowesse, valiancie, cheualrie, and actiuitie, that he not onely herein imitated the examplers of godly K. Dauid for his Israelites as before [the reference here is to the Bow of Promise after the Deluge], and of that noble Emperour Leo in ouerthrowing idolatrie, and exalting archerie maugre the mallice of that Romane Antichrist, and all his members: but also inuincibly maintayned the praiseworthie practize of this shooting in peace & wars by the examples of his princly progenitors. As after the conquest, of K. Henry

II. aliîas Beauclerk so sirnamed, the first furtherer of K. Arthures benificencie, valiāt Edward sirnamed long & first vizitor of the saide Kinges tombe, valiant and victorius Edward III. & IIII. bountious and liberall Richard II. good and gratiouse Henry the V. wise, politique, iust, temperate, and graue King Henry the VII. his father.[83]

Apparently a Prince Arthur's London Round Table enjoyed, save for the strange interlude of Mary I, a continuous existence to the reign of Elizabeth, for Robinson continues:

Neither hath this ceased in the branch, that flourished in the bole: but by the milde, religiouse, and gratiouse King Edwarde the VI. and now last of all by the Phenix of feminine sex, our most redoubted Hester and gratiouse soueraigne Ladie Queene Elizabeth laudably lasteth in force and effect.[84]

The "redoubted Hester" herself helps to substantiate Robinson, for when she chanced to meet a procession of Prince Arthur's Knights set in festive array by the Hugh Offley whom Mulcaster has identified as Sir Lancelot and the "famosest knight" of the order, she gave them her royal commendation:

A little before the year 1588, Hugh Offley, a rich Citizen of London, free of the Leather-sellers' Company,[85] set forth, at his own expence, a costly show of Prince Arthur, with his Knights of the Round Table. He made choice of 300 archers, personable men, and well appointed in black satin doublets and black velvet hose;

every one having a bow of yew and a dozen of waxed arrows. He appointed certain stages and forts and marks to shoot at, with liberal rewards to them that won the prizes, and plentiful banquets for them all. They marched in goodly and orderly array, three together, every three a bow length from the other, from Merchant Taylors' Hall to Mile-end Green. Queen Elizabeth happened to pass by, and she ordered her chariot to be stopped, that she might see the show, and speaking to the Nobility that attended her, said, "that in her life she never saw a more stately company of archers." They, approaching near to her Majesty, did their duty upon their knee, praying God long to prosper and preserve her Majesty; whereupon she most graciously bowed her body, and gave them most hearty thanks, saying, "she would love, maintain, and advance, her Citizens of the City of London;" and so prayed to God to bless all her good subjects therein.[86]

In 1583 Robinson brought out, with a dedication to Elizabeth, a work devoted especially to the "*now famous order of Knightes of Prince* Arthures Round Table *or* Society":

THE AVNCIENT Order, Societie, and Vnitie *L*audable, of *Prince Arthure*, and his knightly Armory of the *Round Table*. With a Threefold Assertion frendly in fauour and furtherance of English Archery at this day.[87]

This work, in which Robinson reasserts the fact that Henry VIII's "Daughter deare. ELIZABETH our Soueraigne QVEENE likewise, Confirmes this Order still, and doth mentaine this exercyse," [88] appears to have been "translated (oute of a litle

frenche booke printed at Parys in Anno Xti
1546)," [89] and was distributed among Prince
Arthur and "his 56 knightes . . . when they shott
under the same Prince Arthure at Myles ende
greene." [90] An earlier edition of the French book
proves to be a sort of text-book on heraldry, *La
deuise Des armes des Cheualiers de la Table ronde*,[91]
taken up almost entirely with the painted coats of
arms of the knights of the Round Table, with appropriate legends in prose beneath. In addition to
"Le Roi Artus," the names of one hundred and
sixty-eight knights, beginning with "Messire
Lancelot du lac," appear above variegated and
multiform escutcheons, all in the shape of shields,
while the last eight escutcheons stand without the
names of knights.[92] The main interest of Robinson's translation is that he adapts the French book
for the purpose of advertising Prince Arthur and
the London Round Table: the French book says
nothing of Arthur's connection with archery. After
some preliminary matter, which Robinson trans-
lates from the French and which is out of place for
his main purpose, he comes "to the Armorie of
Prince ARTHVRE and the KNIGHTS of his Round
Table florishing by the fame of Englishe Archery,
at this daye." [93] Where the French shield for Arthur has thirteen crowns, Robinson's, which he
ascribes to Thomas Smith, has three.[94] Robinson

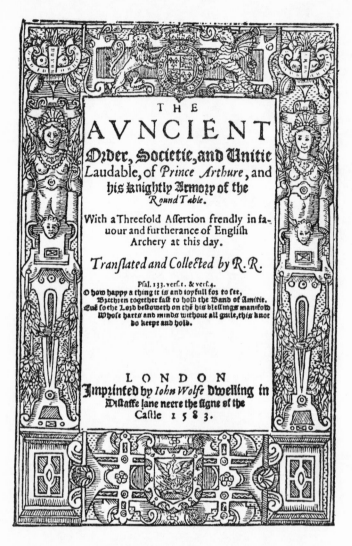

THE
AVNCIENT
Order, Societie, and Unitie
Laudable, of *Prince Arthure*, and
his knightly Armory of the
Round Table.

With a Threefold Aſſertion frendly in fauour and furtherance of Engliſh
Archery at this day.

Tranſlated and Collected by R. R.

Pſal. 133. verſ. 1. & verſ. 4.
O how happy a thing it is and ioyfull for to ſee,
Brethren together faſt to hold the Band of Amitie.
Euk ſo the Lord beſtoweth on this his bleſſings manifold
Whoſe harts and minds without all guile, this knot
do keepe and hold.

LONDON
Imprinted by *Iohn Wolfe* Dwelling in
Diſtaffe lane neere the ſigne of the
Caſtle 1 5 8 3.

Title-page of Richard Robinson's Book in Praise of
Prince Arthur and London's Round Table of Archers.
(British Museum G.11,235.)

ELIZABETH
Hee graunt oure
With longe and
His glorye

(Gods Fulnes)
QVEENE to Raigne
Perfect Blessednes,
to Mentaine.

Prince Arthures Armes for that
Society of Archers in
London.

M. Thomas Smith Cheef Custo-
mar for her Maiesty in the
Port of London.

A Monges praiseworthy Monuments which English KINGES haue made
For maintenaudce of Manly acts, whose Fame shall neuer fade,
King HENRY the 8. hath condigne praise and Princely memory,
(For chusing Knights of ARTHVRES traine to mentaine Archery):
Whose Maiesty at Myle end with his NOBLES vsed this game,
That Citizens and Subiects all might exercise the same.
But specially for CITIZENS hee made this Order theare,
One Cheeftavne chose and certeyn Knights to sport them once a yeare.
His Daughter deare. ELIZABETH our Soueraigne QVEENE likewise,
Confirmes this Order still, and doth mentaine this exercyse
Eche Subiect pray and praise GOD for her long and prosperous Raigne,
Our Bowes in our handes stronger then with Honour shall remaine.

Anno. 1543
S. W. Bow
yer Maior.

Anno. 1544
S. Martin
Bowes.
Maior.
Iob.29.

B

Richard Robinson's *Auncient Order*, 1583, Signature B, Showing
the Dedication to Elizabeth. (British Museum G.11,235.)

begins his series with "S. Lancelot du Lac," and
has fifty-eight shields, numbered continuously,
each surmounted by the name of an Arthurian
knight. There are, of course, not so many shields
as in the French book, and in his selection of
knights Robinson does not follow the French order
exactly. No field is emblazoned either with ar-
morial bearings or with colors, and the form of the
blank shield for each knight is exactly the same.
From the corresponding prose legend of the French,
Robinson adapts a verse legend in two stanzas of
resolved riming septenaries which describe the virtues of the appropriate knight and what emblazon-
ing the blank device ought to contain. Of para-
mount importance, however, is the fact that to the
right and left of all of Robinson's shields, with the
exception of five, are placed initials in roman
capitals, which no doubt refer to members of the
society.[95] This is confirmed by Mulcaster's reference in the *Positions* to "maister *Hewgh Offly*, . . .
my noble fellow in that order Syr *Launcelot*," [96]
and by the initials "H. O." on the page which Robinson devotes to "S. Lancelot du Lac." [97] It is
therefore disappointing not to find the initials
"R. M." by any one of the shields. But we have
"their fellow knight's" own word to vouch for his
membership, and it is possible that Mulcaster's
name as a member, or the name assigned him by

Robinson, was that of one of the knights who have no initials: "Blyomberyes de [Gannes]," "Messire Gaherryet," "Keux le seneschall," "Messire Iuaine," or "S. Bodovier of VVinchelsey."[98]

In 1581 Spenser had been away from Mulcaster's instruction for some twelve years, and was probably in Dublin. Yet it is possible that Mulcaster had become a member of the Society of Archers before Spenser left for Cambridge in 1569, and if not, the significance of his membership nevertheless remains. In any case, Robinson's account of the London Round Table which flourished in memory of Arthur's Table Round and enjoyed the commendation of Elizabeth, helps us to measure the vitality and popularity of Arthurian tradition in Tudor England. Spenser certainly knew of London's Prince Arthur and his Knights of the Round Table — that organization which did not escape the memory of Justice Shallow when Falstaff was enlisting recruits: "I remember at Mile-end Green, when I lay at Clement's Inn, — I was then Sir Dagonet in Arthur's show." [99] To be able to postulate with reasonable assurance that Spenser went to grammar school under the mastership of, say, "Messire Iuaine" Mulcaster, lends living color to *The Faerie Queene*.

In 1569 Spenser entered Cambridge, of which in the fifteenth century Nicholaus Cantalupus, "*a*

¶Messire Lancelot du lac.

¶Messire Lancelot du lac portoit en
ses armes dargēt a trois bēdes de bel-
lif. Il estoit preux/z hardy/z lung des
plus nobles z eminēs de la table rōde
qui ayma a secret la belle Genieure
femme du roy Artus/et feit choses si
admiral les quon a cōpose de luy ung
grāt liure cōtenāt ses faictz et pesses.

*La deuise Des armes des Cheualiers de la Table
ronde*, Paris, [1520?], Signature [a viii^v].
(British Museum 607.a.24.)

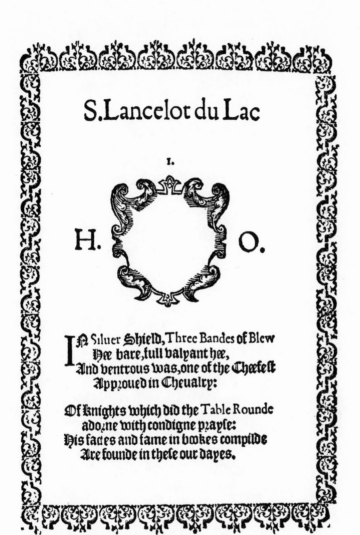

S. Lancelot du Lac

I.

H.　　　　O.

IN Siluer Shield, Three Bandes of Blew
　　Hee bare, full valyant hee,
And ventrous was, one of the Cheefest
　　Approued in Cheualry:

Of knights which did the Table Rounde
　　adozne with condigne prayse:
His faces and fame in bookes compilde
　　Are founde in these our dayes.

Richard Robinson's *Auncient Order*, 1583, Signature B^v, Showing
Robinson's Metrical Adaptation of the French Prose and the
Initials of Hugh Offley, the Sir Lancelot of the London Round
Table.　(British Museum G.11,235.)

Welch *Gentleman*," had claimed Arthur as a founder
to offset the Alfredian tradition of Oxford. Cantalupus went so far as to state that Arthur appointed one "Kynotus" Rector of Cambridge, and
he gave the text of a charter which he stated that
Arthur transmitted "per suum nepotem Walwanum." [100] The fact that in 1568 the master of a
Cambridge college reasserted the Arthurian foundation of the university shows the tenacity of
Arthurian tradition during Spenser's apprentice
period. In that year John Caius [101]— Padua M.D.,
sometime royal physician to Edward VI, Mary I,
and Elizabeth, and from 1559 to 1573 Master of
Gonville and Caius College — brought out anony-
mously his *De antiquitate Cantabrigiensis Academiae Libri duo*, to which he subjoined, also anony-
mously, a dissertation by Thomas Caius [102] on the
antiquity of Oxford — *Assertio antiquitatis Oxoniensis Academiae, incerto Authore* — addressed to
Elizabeth. One story has it that the controversy
grew out of Elizabeth's visit to Cambridge on
August 9, 1564, during which William Masters,
public orator, made the assertion that Cambridge
was a more ancient university than Oxford. Masters' assertion became known to Thomas Caius,
who then wrote his defence of Oxford. John Caius,
in turn, found a manuscript copy of Thomas
Caius's defence in the Earl of Leicester's library,

and published it, without inquiring after the author, as an appendix to his own championing of Masters and Cambridge. Thomas Caius's second defence remained in manuscript during the controversy.[103] In 1574 — both the champions were then dead — during the fifth year of Spenser's residence at Cambridge, the 1568 edition was reprinted at the instruction of Archbishop Parker, with the author's name on the title-page and with an addendum by him, *Historiae Cantebrigiensis Academiae ab vrbe condita* [*Libri duo*]. The several issues of this second edition vary greatly.

An attempt to unravel all the lines of argument in the several books mentioned would be irrelevant here. Suffice it to say that both John and Thomas quote extensively from the Arthurian chroniclers and that Thomas, in his answer to Masters' claim, reaffirms the tradition that Oxford was founded by King Alfred — "ab optimo pariter & doctissimo principe Alphredo, qui & Aluredus dicitur." [104] This, John Caius denies, and brings to the support of Cambridge supposed favors from the hands of Kings Lucius, Sigebert, and others, and "diploma illud magni regis Arthuri, quod subsequitur." [105] He then quotes, with a few slight changes, the text of the forged charter as given by Nicholaus Cantalupus, omitting the subsequent statement that Arthur sent the charter to Kynotus by Gawain.[106]

After commending Leland's *Assertio* for proof of
the historicity of Arthur, and after dubbing Polydore Vergil a man who "ita & hîc licentèr errat,"[107]
John Caius goes on to say:

> Redeo ad Arthurum, cuius historiam vehementer
> laudo. Excipio quasdam aniles fabulas, quas Gul. Noui-
> burgensis in prooemio, & Henr. Marleburgensis[108] suo
> damnat in libro, cùm alioqui dignus Arthurus erat,
> quem veraces historiae praedicarent, vt idem Marle-
> burgensis censet, quòd labentem patriam sustinuerit,
> infractos ciuium animos ad bellum acuerit, multas re-
> giones Britanniae subiugauerit, . . . & alia multa egregiè
> gesta perpetrauerit. Fabulas enim volo tolli, non per-
> sonam. . . . Audio etiā in Arce Londinēsi inter regni
> vetustas cōcessionum tabulas atq3 monumenta, su-
> peresse adhuc vetus scriptum, quod iurisconsulti vocant,
> Inspeximus, in quo Arthuri concessionum Cantebri-
> giensi Academiae mentio est.[109]

In his manuscript answer Thomas Caius, who errs
as much in defence of Alfred, adjudges Arthur's
diploma to be "fictum & adulterinum."[110] But the
rumor of the Arthurian "privilege" was nevertheless in the Elizabethan air. Leland had apparently
heard of it before 1544, as is evidenced by *A
Learned and True Assertion*:

> There is also (if we may beleeue credible reporte) in
> the treasuries at *Cambridge* at this daye, a Table of the
> priuiledge by *Arthure* sometime confirmed to the fur-
> derāce of studēts. But as yet haue I not searched out
> the credite of this deede.[111]

And Robinson's added parenthesis of 1582 is of further significance.

From the point of view of authenticity, John would probably have done better if he had stuck to his treatises on "Sweatyng Sicknesse" or "Englishe Dogges," and Thomas to his Latin epigrams, but let us reserve our judgment of Thomas, and for John substitute that of a literary historian of the following century:

> The most learn'd *Cantabrigian* Antiquary that has yet appear'd was *John Caius.* . . . His two Books . . . *De Antiquitate Cantabrigiensis Academiae* were written, in defence of the *Cambridge*-Orator, against *Tho. Key.* . . . His first Attempt is to establish the lately advanc'd Doctrin of his Mother's great Age and Seniority; which he endeavours to do from the exemplify'd Charters of King *Arthur* and King *Cadwallader*, together with those of the Popes *Honorius* and *Sergius.* This done, his next Business is to overthrow the pretended Antiquity of *Oxford*; which (in his second Book) he dispatches as effectually as he had done his former Argument.[112]

We have, therefore, damned John Caius with faint praise; but the significant fact remains that Spenser happened to be in residence at a university which already had over a century of Arthurian tradition behind it, at the very time when it aligned itself behind Arthur to the extent of open controversy. In a supposed letter to Spenser, Gabriel Harvey refers to the first edition of John Caius's book by praising "the trim lattin phrases and witty proverbes of him that built Caius College and made Londinensis Booke de Antiquitate," [113] and Spenser himself in *The Faerie Queene* shows which side he was on when he refers to the students of "my mother Cambridge" as Oxford's "elder sisters broode." [114]

Robinson's *Learned and True Assertion* had, of course, given Leland's defence of Geoffrey of Monmouth to a wider circle of readers, and John Caius's slur on Polydore Vergil shows that the sensibilities of loyal Britons were thoroughly aroused by the logic of a foreigner. All through Spenser's college days, in fact, and on through the publication of *The Faerie Queene* in 1590 and 1596, the defence of Geoffrey's Brutus and Arthur continued.

In 1573 Humphrey Lhuyd's *Commentarioli Britannicae Descriptionis Fragmentum* (Cologne, 1572) [115] was englished by Thomas Twyne, with a dedication to Edward de Vere, Earl of Oxford, under the following title:

The Breuiary of Britayne. As this most noble, and renowmed Iland, was of auncient *time deuided into three King*domes, England, Scotland and Wales, Contaynyng a learned discourse of the variable state, & alteration therof, vnder diuers, as wel natural: as forren princes, & Conquerours. Together with the Geographicall description of the same, such as nether by elder, nor later writers, the like hath been set foorth before.

With Lhuyd the attack on Polydore Vergil takes
on a broader aspect. Lhuyd heaps vitriol on Polydore himself, "infamis homunculus," [116] and on
William of Newburgh and Gildas,[117] and pins "the
liyng champion of the *Scottysh* name, *Hector
Boëthius*" [118] to the list of enemies to the Britons.
Polydore and Hector Boece are thus grouped together:

> When I chaunced of late yeres, to come to the sight
> of *Polydorus Virgilius* the Italian, and *Hector Boethius*
> the *Scot*, their British histories, wherof the first mayn-
> fully sought, not onely to obscure the glory of y̆ British
> name, but also to defame the *Britaynes* themselues with
> sclandrous lies. The other while he goeth about to rayse
> his *Scots* out of darknesse, and obscuritie, what euer he
> findeth that the *Romanes*, or *Britaynes*, haue doone
> worthy cōmendation in this Ilande: all that he attrib-
> uteth vnto his *Scottes*, like a foolish writer.[119]

Lhuyd is thereby "prouoked" and comes to
"guard" his "sweet country from suche incon-
ueniences" [120] imposed by the "slaunderers and
detractours of the *British* glory." [121] Leland himself, whom Lhuyd styles "noster Lelandus," [122]
had called Polydore a successor to "Gulielmus
Paruus" (*i. e.*, William of Newburgh) and had
inveighed likewise against Hector Boece and the
denunciatory epistle of Gildas. John Caius had
continued the attack on Polydore and William of
Newburgh. During the years that intervened be-

tween Leland and Caius and Lhuyd, though the
underlying motive of the defence of Geoffrey of
Monmouth remained the same, the spirit of the defence grew in intensity and broadened in scope, and
Polydore did not invariably bear the brunt of the
attack. The attitude of Scotland, whose Highland
Scots were as Briton as the Welsh of Wales, is indicative of a change that had come over Geoffrey's
"rex Britanniae" since the days of the Angevin
dynasty and before a Tudor had ever sat on the
throne of England.

The Angevin exploitation of Arthur as a national, an English, hero, and the appeal for the
suzerainty of Scotland on the basis of the overlord-
ship of British kings as chronicled by Geoffrey of
Monmouth — Edward I cited the tenure of Augu-
selus as Arthur's vassal [123] — served to check whatever Scottish interest there may have been in the
Celtic Messiahship of Arthur, and Merlin was
forced to yield some of his prophetic powers to
Thomas of Erceldoune.[124] The Scots denounced
Brutus, forsook the bastard Arthur, and recognized
Mordred (son of King Loth), whom they appro-
priated as a Scottish hero, as the legitimate heir to
the throne of Uther Pendragon. In his difficulties
with Scotland, Henry VIII also appealed to the
status of ancient British kings for his sovereign
right, asserting to his "Nephieu the kyng of Scot-

tis" that "the kynges of Scottes haue always knowl-
edged the kynges of Englande superior lordes of
the realme of Scotlande, and haue done homage
and fealtie for the same." [125] There was no Scottish enthusiasm, therefore, over the Welsh House
of Tudor, and the marriage of Margaret, Henry's
sister, to James IV of Scotland did not prevent the
traditional enmity from flaming at Flodden Field
in 1513 and yet again at Solway Moss in 1542.[126]
James VI considered *The Faerie Queene* not so
much a glorification of Elizabeth Tudor as a libel
on his mother, Mary Queen of Scots.[127] It was only
with the "Scottish Englishing" [128] in 1603, if then,
that to Scotland the blood of a Tudor princess became thicker than water.

Hector Boece, the Aberdeen "Scholemayster,"
had therefore taken the typically Scottish attitude
in his *Scotorum Historia* (1527), the conflicting sen-
timents of which Lhuyd dubs as "starke lies," such
"as neither *Lucian* in his *Fabulous narrations*,
neither the author of the booke of *Amadis* of *Gaule*,
nor wittie ARIOSTVS in his *Orlando Furioso*,
haue euer commended vnto vs in Fables." [129]
Lhuyd's typical attitude may be summed up in his
words on Arthur:

Britayne hath also brought foorth to the worlde the
moste puissant, and inuincible kynge, *Arthur*, whose
euerlastynge renowme, and most noble deedes: our

freende Mayster *Leland*, hath set foorthe, and made
more apparant by infinite testimonies, and moste
weightie argumentes agaynst the gnarrynge, and dog-
gysh mouthe, and hatred more then euer was *Vatinians*,
of *Polydorus Vrbine*, and of the gresie Monke *Rhicual-
lensis*, more conuersant in the kitchin, then in the hystories of olde writers.

And not only our countrymen: but also *Spayniardes*,
Italians, *Frenchmen*, and the *Sueones*, beyonde the Sea
Baltheum, (as *Gothus* reporteth out of their Hystories)
doo celebrate, and aduance vnto this day, in theyr
bookes the worthy actes of this puissant kyng.[130]

Commendatory verses in praise of Lhuyd by
Edward Grant, the biographer of Ascham, are
enough to show the spirit in which the substance of
the translation and the Latin original was received
by the general run of the Britons:

> By whose endeuour *Polidore*,
>   must now sursease to prate,
> To forge, to lie, and to defame,
>   kynge *BRVTVS* worthy state.
> By whose great paynes, proude *Hector* Scot,
>   must now leaue of to bable,
> Such vaunts: as of his Scottish soyle,
>   he whilom seemd to fable.
> By *Lhuid* their brags be beaten downe,
>   their forgyng lies be spide,
> And *Britaine* needs must chaleng fame
>   that erst it was denide.
>
>   .   .   .   .
>
> *Brutes* worthy race is blazed here,
>   by trumpe of flickering fame:
> And *Lhuid*, it is a flowyng flud,
>   that hath reuiude the same.

Who, though enterred now in earthe
    yet shall he neuer die,
But liue amongs his *Britanists*,
    by this his *Britanie*.[131]

Gabriel Harvey possessed a copy of *The Breuiary* on the title-page of which he wrote: "Tractatus, cuique Anglo necessarius; non ignoranti, rudique suae patriae." [132] Hubert Languet, whose reflections are especially interesting because they occur in a letter to Sidney, represents both the foreign and the learned attitude toward Lhuyd. Languet writes from Vienna on January 28, 1574, calling particular attention to one of "two most charming writers" whom he has recently come upon — the one who "repeatedly proclaims himself a Cambrian, not an Englishman":

His name is Humfrey Lhuid, and if he is not learned, he is a man of extensive reading, but now and then forms his judgements in such a way that he seems totally destitute of common sense. He scourges the unfortunate Hector Boetius and Polydore Virgil so cruelly that even if they have grievously erred, the punishment 'seems greater than the fault. . . . Some of the Germans had left us [*i. e.*, the French] the incendiary Brennus, in consideration of his sacrilege and horrible death; but he takes him away from us and makes him a Welshman. . . . I had gone on half asleep reading my good Welshman till very late at night; and somehow or other it fell out that the flame of my lamp caught the book, and before I could put the fire out, it was well-nigh burnt up, for it was not bound. I was distressed at first, but when

I recovered myself I began to laugh, and reflected that
it was a good thing for me, as it deprived me of the occasion of wasting my time on such follies.[133]

Languet adds that he was on the point of sending
Sidney the scorched remains in order that Sidney's
Welsh servant Griffin might perform Lhuyd's obse-
quies while Sidney himself offered a laugh to appease the ghost. In his reply from Padua on
February 11 Sidney refers jestingly to "our poor
Cambro-Briton": "Griffin had a good deal to say in
memory of Master Lhuid, and made him a sort of
funeral oration, while I appeased his ghost with a
hearty laugh." [134]

In 1573 Richard Price published, with a dedication to Lord Burghley, the *Historiae Brytannicae
Defensio*,[135] an earlier written work by his father,
Sir John Price (ap Rhys), addressed to Edward VI
and to William Herbert, Earl of Pembroke. In his
dedicatory epistle to Burghley, he praises Leland,
Bale, John Caius ("in eleganti illo de Cantabrigiae
antiquitate libello"), and Lhuyd,[136] and places his
father in the patriotic succession of loyal Britons:

Ioannes etiam Priseus pater meus, amplitudini tuae
(vt opinor) non ignotus, in hoc diligenter cum alijs in-
cumbens, vt historiae Brytannicae veritas à Polydoro
oppugnata, sarta & tecta seruaretur, ante annos xx.[137]

By and large, Sir John defends the authenticity of
Geoffrey of Monmouth against the strictures of

Polydore Vergil; yet he stresses also the antiquity of Geoffrey. Once more Geoffrey is not "Author," but "Interpres" of the *Historia*. Sir John devotes one section of his defence to a vindication of the historicity of Arthur (*De Arthuro Brytonum Rege illustrissimo* [138]), and still another to probable conjectures as to why Gildas failed to mention Arthur.[139] His point of departure against Polydore Vergil is shown by the opening sentence of the former section:

Etsi Polydorus ipse, hunc apertè ex Regum Brytannorum catalogo non reijciat, adeò vt quibusdam simplicioribus, qui in ipsius historiae lectionem incidunt, immeritò inter eos qui Arthurum impugnent, censendus esse videatur, obliquè tamen ipsius famae & gloriae immortali detrahere deprehenditur.[140]

In 1576 William Lambard set apart a section of his *Perambulation of Kent* to a consideration of the ancient British history. In "A short counsell, as touching the Bryttishe hystorie," [141] he says he is "iustly occasioned" to turn aside from his county history to speak "for confirmation of the credite of oure *Bryttishe* or *Welshe hystorie*, (the faith wherof is by *William Petite* [*i. e.*, William of Newburgh], and *Polydore Virgile* called into question)." Lambard continues:

The state of the matter is this, whether *Geffray* of *Monmouthe* be the authour of the *Bryttish* storie (as

William Newborow, and *Polydore* charge him) or the *translatour* thereof onely out of the *Bryttishe*, as him selfe in his booke professeth.[142]

Lambard believes that the matter of debate has already found "more learned and diligent *Patrones*," and he urges his readers to go to Leland and Price ("ap Rese") for more detailed information. He carries Bale's and Price's point of view one step farther: he would attest the antiquity of Geoffrey's substance, and not necessarily the verity of every word. Thus Polydore Vergil comes in for not so much censure as before, for

if he shall seeke to discredit the whole worke, for that in some partes it conteineth matter, not only vnlikely, but incredible also: then shall he bothe depriue this Nation of all manner of knowledge of their first beginning, and open the way for vs also to cal into question the origine, and antiquities of *Spaine, Fraunce, Germanie*, yea and of *Italie* his owne countrie: in which, that whiche *Liuie* reporteth of *Romulus* and *Remus*, *Numa* and *Aegeria*, is as farre remoued from all suspicion of truthe, as any thing, whatsoeuer ẏ *Galfride* writeth, either of *Brute, Merlin*, or *King Arthur* himselfe.[143]

But Lambard is genuinely patriotic, and his point of view, though it is altogether the common-sense one — "any wryter of the auncient hystorie of any nation" has "his propre vanities mixed with sincere veritie"[144] — shows him to be a loyal supporter of the attack launched by Leland.

In 1584 David Powel brought out an edition
(with alterations) of Lhuyd's English translation
of the *Brut* attributed to Caradoc of Llancarvan:
"The historie of Cambria, now called Wales: *A
part of the most fa*mous Yland of Brytaine, *written
in the Brytish lang*uage aboue two hundreth *yeares
past: translated into* English by H. Lhoyd *Gentleman:* Corrected, augmented, *and continued out of
Re*cords and best approoued *Authors.*" [145]   The
edition, which also contains Lhuyd's version of Sir
John Price's *Description of Cambria,* [146] was published at the request of Sir Henry Sidney, sometime
Lord President of Wales, and is dedicated to Sir
Philip. Powel states that in preparing the edition
he procured all the authors that he "could come by,
which haue anie thing written of the affaires of
VVales," and his enumeration of Geoffrey, William
of Newburgh, Polydore Vergil, Leland, Bale, Price,
John Caius, and Lambard shows him to be another
champion of the Britons.[147]   In *A Description of
Cambria,* "*Polydore Virgil* with an *Italian* brag" is
reproved:

Polydore did either neuer see nor read the ancient
histories of this realme, or dissembleth the same to the
aduancement and praise of himselfe and his countrie.
. . . He being first a straunger borne, and also ignorant
as well in the histories of this realme, as of those toongs
and languages wherin the same were written, could
neuer set foorth the true and perfect Chronicle of the
same.[148]

In the conclusion of his book Powel goes out of his way to connect the Sidneys with "*Ednyuet Vachan*, chéefe counseller and steward to *Lhewelyn ap Iorwerth* Prince of *Wales*, . . . who also was the auncestor of *Owen Tuder*, the Grandfather of king *Henrie* the seuenth." [149]

Furthermore, Powel's assertion of the claim of the sovereignty of the Prince of North Wales over the Princes of South Wales and Powis quickened an argument among the Welsh which had been rife since long before the time of the Edwardian conquest, and which may well have influenced the geography and topography of *The Faerie Queene*. The nature and extent of the controversy is revealed by Robert Vaughan's book of 1662: "British Antiquities revived: Or A friendly Contest touching the *soveraignty* of the *three* Princes of *VVales* in ancient times, managed with certain *arguments*, whereunto *answers* are applyed." Vaughan states that the contentions of the Southwallians were delivered to him by Sir John Lloyd about forty years previous, and explains that the writing of his book

was upon this *occasion*: some Gentlemen of *Southwales* being dissatisfied with *Caradoc of Lancarvan's* History of *Wales*, published by *Dr. Powel*, in regard that therein the Prince of *Northwales* is held forth to be *Soveraigne* over the other two princes of *Southwales* and *Powis*, as being of the elder house, thought fit (in order to the compiling of a more *exact history*) to draw up certain arguments for the *soveraignty* of all *Wales* to be in the Prince of *Southwales*, and to send them also into *Northwales* to see what could be said in answer to them, before any further use should be made of them.[156]

The sixth argument of the Southwallians is that the English based their title to Wales on the conquering of Rhys ap Tudor in the reign of William Rufus, and not on the conquering of Llewelyn ap Griffith in the reign of Edward I; that Rhys was looked upon as an enemy and given an honorable burial, whereas Llewelyn was regarded as a rebel and his body was treated with shame. Vaughan, however, says he aims at the *truth*. He reaches the general conclusion that "the *Princes* of *Northwales* had the *soveraignty* over all *Wales*," [151] and affirms North Wales to be "the soveraign seat of the *Britains*." [152] So it was in the days of Spenser, for, according to Lhuyd, "in *Northwales*, the *welshmen*, keepe their olde boundes." [153]

In 1585 Powel brought out an edition of Ponticus Virunnius' Latin prose condensation of Geoffrey's *Historia*,[154] in the dedicatory letter of which to Sir Henry Sidney he recognizes that the question of Arthur's historicity is the chief bone of contention in the attack on Polydore Vergil:

Nihilominus tamen manifestum est, cum ex multis antiquis monumentis quae ab Arthuro denominationem sortita sunt, tùm etiam ex historijs Scoticis & Saxonicis, & doctissimorum virorum scriptis, qui historiam illam

defendunt, hunc Arthurum, Britanniae regem, atque
virum bellica laude praestantem fuisse, rebùsque prae-
clarè gestis saepius de hostibus triumphasse.[155]

Polydore Vergil and George Buchanan are classed
among writers "externi & rerum Britannicarum
insolentes." [156] But Powel is altogether sensible in
answer to those who would refuse the fables and
errors of Geoffrey on the authority of William of
Newburgh:

> Si quae eius temporis verior & contestatior haberi
> possit historia, producatur in medium, admittatur, re-
> tineatur. Deinde ad Neubrigensis authoritatem in con-
> trarium adductam, hoc tantum dico: eius fidem mihi
> hac in re non probari.[157]

There is no need to let Powel give vent to all his
spleen when Thomas Churchyard is quite willing
to talk about him.

Thomas Churchyard in *The Worthines of Wales*
(1587), which he dedicated to Elizabeth, begins by
saying that he wishes to be free from "such cauel-
ing," and he uses Powel as his example:

> Dauid Powell a late writer, yet excellently learned,
> made a sharp inuectiue against William Paruus and
> Pollidor Virgill (& all their complices) accusing them of
> lying tongues, enuyous detraction, malicious slaunders,
> reproachfull and venomous language, wilfull ignorāce,
> dogged enuie, and canckered mindes, for that thei
> spake vnreuerently of Arthur, and many other thrise
> noble Princes.[158]

But Churchyard cannot refrain from digressing from "the orderly matter of the booke" to "touch somewhat the workes and wordes of them that rashly haue written more then they knewe, or well could proue":

> As learned men, hath wrote graue works of yore,
> So great regard, to natiue Soyle they had:
> For such respect, I blame now *Pollydore*:
> Because of *Wales*, his iudgment was but bad.
> If *Buckanan*, the *Scottish* Poet late
> Were here in sprite, of *Brittons* to debate:
> He should finde men, that would with him dispute,
> And many a pen, which would his works confute.
>
> .   .   .   .
>
> And trueth I trowe, is likte among vs best:
> For each man frounes, when fabling toyes they heare,
> And though we count, but *Robin Hood* a Iest,
> And old wiues tales, as tatling toyes appeare:
> Yet *Arthurs* raigne, the world cannot denye,
> Such proofe there is, the troth thereof to trye:
> That who so speakes, against so graue a thing,
> Shall blush to blot, the fame of such a King.[159]

Churchyard then englishes several passages of Geoffrey's *Historia* from one of the two editions by Jodocus Badius Ascensius,[160] and in Arthur's defiance of Lucius he recognizes England's independence of Rome.

In 1575, the year before Spenser was graduated M.A., he no doubt met Richard Harvey, a younger brother of his friend Gabriel Harvey. Richard entered Pembroke Hall in that year, and, significantly enough, published in 1593 — with an explanatory note to his brother Gabriel and a dedication to Robert Devereux, Earl of Essex — his *Philadelphus, or a Defence of Brutes, and the Brutans History*.[161] If human nature has not violently changed in three hundred and fifty odd years, we do not have to tax our imaginations (especially when we remember also John Caius's tract) to postulate relevant discussions among the Cambridge students with Spenser in the midst of them. Harvey's little book, following Powel's attack and Churchyard's suggestion, is directed specifically against George Buchanan's *Rerum Scoticarum Historia* (1582), and shows a further extension of the assault on Polydore Vergil. Buchanan is mentioned several times in *A Veue of the Present State of Ireland* [162] — once with the citation "Buckanan *de rebus Scoticis*" [163] — and in one place Irenæus questions Buchanan's reliability:

Buckhanan, for that he himselfe, beinge an Irishe Scott or Picte by nacon, and beinge very excellently learned, and industrious to seeke out the truth of these thinges concerninge the originall of his owne people, hath both sett downe the testimonies of the auncyents truly, and his owne opinion withall very reasonablie, though in some thinges he doth somewhat flatter.[164]

It is of interest that Harvey compliments Elizabeth by alluding to *The Faerie Queene*:

Yet infinite be that time, which is predestinated for the name of *Brute* and his *Brutans*, euerlasting be that

honor which is due to the branches of such a Tree as
groweth without withering, is strong without decay, and
may best serue euen for the *Phenix* of all men, and *Vna*
of all the women in the earth.[165]

The allusion is to the heroine of Book I, and pays
Spenser a unique compliment at the time when
Shakspere's Julia was holding the stage, and just
before Juliet and Bassanio's Portia were to step
upon the scene.

In his dedication to Essex, Spenser's supposed
last patron, Harvey begins his "mightie Captaines
present defence" by stating:

I hope, I am cleane from any abuse in this present
treatise, I will euer honour strangers, for their good
qualities of learning and life: but I must not hold my
hand and pen still, when I see them too busie, in tossing
our histories and actes, at their owne pleasure, which
appertaine not vnto them: they cannot stay mee from
my studie, more then I kept them from this practise.
I fauour the historie of *Brute*, without regard of their
disfauour, as they dislike it, without respect of other
mens liking. I cannot in loyaltie defend euery *Brute*,
but I may without any breach of dutie, defend this
great *Brute of Brutanie*.[166]

To "His Most Louing Brother, Master Gabriell
Haruey," he writes:

When I saw, both how *iestingly*, and *seriously* our
Historie of *Brute* was reiected of some auncient and
newe bookmen, I tried their maruellous *iestes* and *rea-*
sons, and felt them too weake to moue me. Now my

PHILADELPHVS,

OR

A Defence of Brutes, and the Brutans History.

Written by R. H.

Imprinted at London by Iohn Wolfe. 1593.

Title-page of Richard Harvey's Tract in Defence of Brutus
and the Descendants of Brutus against George
Buchanan's *Rerum Scoticarum Historia*, 1582.
(British Museum G.5932.)

Answere is on foot with their Reply, I may iustly hold
mine owne, and stand on *Brutes* side against all chal-
lengers that are or will come. I saye, Puissant *Brute* is
no *fabulous Prince*, but a true example, no counterfeit
man, but a corporall possessor of this Iland; let them
saye what they can.[167]

Harvey begins his tract proper with "A Defence
of Brutes Historie":

Master *Buchanan*, though some call you the trumpet
of *Scotland*, and some the noble Scholler, yet I will be so
bold, as answere your larum, touching the history of
mighty *Brute*: because your inuectiue treatise, is in
trueth, more factious, then effectuall. You and such
hotbraines, haue deuised a faction, and diuorcement of
opinions, (I dare say) without fruit, and I beleeue, without cause: For my part, your deniall is not able once to
moue me, and your reasons against *Brutes* historie, shall
neuer perswade any sufficient reader, to agree with you,
and remoue the markes and circuites, that *Geffry Monmouth* hath set downe.[168]

Affirming that "we are not *Brittons*, we are *Brutans*," [169] Harvey continues:

You may easily say, *A Moonke was the deuiser of this
Brute*, you will say, that *he played the Poet*, that hee
carued & painted him in this maner: but you cannot yet
proue in this hast, that *the Moonke* or student had not
good proofe in his readings of this *Brute*, that he had
not his Authour for them. It is out of question, that
manie books haue been written but once, and that many
such singular bookes haue been lost for want of coppies,
and it is probable, that this *Moonke* had some olde
monument or booke, which may bee in *Cambry* to this

day, though *Buchanan* and *Liuy* neuer heard of it, and
may be as true of *Brute*, as their olde *Scottish Thinges*
and Romish Decades are accounted true by their
fauourers and countrimen.[170]

In answer to Buchanan's statement that the ancient Briton speech was not the same as that then
in use in Wales, Harvey says:

Yet by your leaue, *Buchanan*, it is no proofe against
this language, in that *many tongues appeare in it* in your
time, seeing *Brutanisme* might at first bee as full of
diuerse *tongues* by reason of much trauell as it is nowe,
and then your argument hath nor vse nor force in your
question: and in trueth, though *Scots* be called generally
false, yet *Buchanan* may be true; so *Moonks* may *dreame
dreames*, and yet *Geffry Monmouth* write a trueth.
Why should not a *Moonke* be as credible as a *Pædanty?*
or a solitarie student vnderstand that he readeth as
much as a busie schoolemaster? or a *Cambrian* read
Chronicles which a *Scot* neuer saw? or *Geffry* be as plaine
and verifiable as *Buchanan*, being not so deep ouer head
and eares in verses and *Poetry* as he? . . . Thus it cannot
be proued euidently, that *the history of Brute is a* fained
and *poeticall narration*, vnlesse it be first proued, that
there were no more Intelligences and Registers in the
life of *Geffrey* then of *George*, and that *Geffrey* had no
Authours for his defence, because *George* cannot knowe
them. . . .

When *Brutans* haue published *an Historie* and allowed it a long time, we would not haue a *Scot* so pre-
sumptuous, as to *controll* it, much lesse to *reiect* it, as
this one *Scot* hath done very rawly and vnaduisedly.[171]

Polydore Vergil, as we should expect, comes in for
his share of discredit along with Buchanan:

We haue not anything heere for *Italians*, till wee be serued our selues, we are onely in *Brutanie* and among Brutans. . . .

Yet neyther seuen *Polydores* more, nor ten *Buchanans* shall perswade me, that this Genealogy [of "the eighteene Rulers that came of *Brute*"] is a fabulous Tale. Let *Polydore* get him to *Vrbin* in *Italy*, and *Buchanan* hye him to *Buchany* in *Scotland*: it becommeth not these outlandish intruders to vsurpe the censure of the *Brutan* Histories: if they looke well about them they haue enough to doe at home: we neede none of their gossiping cups: but they are dead, and their historicall iudgementes are interred with them: . . . . A *Brutan* may iustly except against the witnesse of an *Italian*, or a *Scot*: Ielousie and malignity are two blinde guids: Then hold your owne, ye braue *Brutans*, and guide your selues, your owne heades are fittest for your owne bodies. . . .

If I omit some histories of Saxons, I do but my duetie: what haue I to do with them, vnlesse it were to make them tributary to *Brutans?* Otherwise, let their owne men commend them if they wil, I owe them no seruice by writing or speaking. Yet I haue named some of the Saxons, though I doe it more for their sakes with whome they dwelt, then for any merite of their owne. Let them lye in dead forgetfulnesse like stones, that haue desired, or doe desire the trouble of *Brutanie*: let their names be cleane put out, and not come among the righteous. . . . Arise ye sonnes of *Ebranke*, and yee kinsmen of true auncient *Brutans*, and make those stonehearted creatures know, that they are made to be your seruants and drudges: let not any double forked toong perswade you, that *Brutanie* is vnder any part of the earth.[172]

Harvey concludes his defence of Brutus by saying:

It is a dangerous position to refuse the offspring of *Brute*, both in regard of all reuerend antiquities of historie, and in respect of our owne Countreimen and neighbours, to whome I wishe all concord and agreement among themselues and against their enemies for euer.[173]

Of the special topics which Harvey discusses, Arthur figures as the most famous king in the "offspring" of Brutus. Harvey stresses Arthur's "Magnificence and Magnanimitie," [174] and under the head of "Victories" the reference to Arthur in connection with some one of the numerous pamphlet-wars of the time, among which Harvey himself was engaged, again verifies the currency and popularity of the Arthurian legend in all the walks of Elizabethan life:

Arthur slew in one day an hundred and fortie Saxons with his owne hand. . . . Now armies stay in Saxony, and papermen flye from those coastes: these do more harme in many places then those old armies did: these will be sauced as they were, and hunted out of the land by order of discipline: none so busie as they, and yet none more slight then they: there is an *Arthur* in paperworke against their inuasions, which may in all right and equitie giue them twelue disgraces at the least, and perhaps twelue times twelue: let the triall proue all, or let that labour be lost, if they can recouer there 12 losses of this newe *Arthur*.[175]

The vital significance of Harvey's tract is therefore apparent, not merely because it has never before been stressed in relation to the Tudor defence of Geoffrey of Monmouth, nor only because its juxtaposition with Spenser has heretofore been overlooked, but also because it illustrates better than any other single document the extent to which Tudor "Brutanisme" reacted to the skepticism against the historicity of Brutus and Arthur. We have not been unfair to Harvey's logic in selecting for illustration the most controversial parts of his argument, for he by no means kept his promise to Essex to be "cleane from any abuse." Harvey is a sworn brother of Leland, Kelton, Lhuyd, and Powel, and he should have been a warm friend to John Dee. With Buchanan's "Brutus parricida" rankling in his ears, to him all enemies to the story of Brutus and his offspring become "Saxons," and the rules of *porcus iste* prevailed. At approximately the date of the publication of the first three books of *The Faerie Queene*, England's "Brutans" are pitted against the four corners of the earth.[176]

The diatribe of Harvey, however, was not the summation of the attitude toward the ancient British history in Spenser's day. But when we find Sir Henry Savile, in his *Rerum Anglicarum Scriptores post Bedam Praecipui* (1596), bringing indecencies to words against Polydore, "vt homo Italus," [177] it is almost high time to call a halt. Except for the scholarly John Twyne, the cau-

tious William Lambard, and the joking Sidney,
William Camden, who remained outside the heat
of controversy, was perhaps the first sixteenth-
century Englishman seriously to approach the
ranks of the skeptics. In his *Britannia* (1586–
1607), Camden was content to survey the prospect,
naming "Viues,[178] Polidorus, Bodinus," [179] "Iohannes de Wheathamsted," [180] "Hadr. Iunius," [181] Buchanan, Boccaccio,[182] and others [183] as opposers.
Camden's failure to declare openly for Geoffrey
brought him in for adverse criticism at the hands of
Edmund Howes, a rather dispassionate partisan,
who edited the 1615 edition of John Stow's *Annales*: "The most learned and diligent Antiquary
master *Cambden* for his own censure doth not denie
the person of *Brute* but relateth the opinions of
others." [184]

The defence of Howes is mainly on behalf of
Brutus, but that it involves Arthur is shown by
the statement that "*Pollidor Virgill* is the onely
man I find, who . . . reiecteth the whole history of
Brute and his successors." Howes also includes as
enemies William of Newburgh and John of Whethamstede, whom he considers "the first that I finde
directly to oppugne the history of *Brute*," adding,
"I do not read of many of our owne that agree
with him, but *Polidor*, *Bodin* and other strangers."[185] He then names, among others who have

"affirmed the Britane history," Leland, Bale, Price, Lambard, and Powel.

The view of Howes is mainly a repetition of Stow's own view in "A Briefe Proofe of *Brute*," [186] which likewise appeared in the 1615 edition of the *Annales*. Stow also probably had his weather-eye on Camden. He makes an appeal for the ancient British history in the name of English patriotism, although he cannot "precisely defend" every detail of the story. As impugners, he mentions, besides John of Whethamstede, William "Petit"— "a French man borne as his name importeth, who most sharply inuayeth not against *Brute*, but against *Galfridus Monmouthensis*, calling him the forger of the British history" [187] — and Polydore Vergil — "an Italian though learned, yet with a vaine glorious enuie to aduance his own country, [who] will not endure that any other country shall haue monuments of antiquitie. And whereas the rest onely except against *Brute*, this man with one dash of a pen cashireth threescore Princes together, with all their histories and historians yea and some Lawes also." [188] Stow groups together "Boccas, Viues, Iunius, Buchanan, Bodin" as "vnfitte to be witnesses in this case, seeing it cannot bee presumed they had any vnderstanding of the English tongue & much lesse of the Welsh." He considers the authority of the ancient British history "setled and approued," and refers the reader to Leland, Price, Lambard, and others.

But we need not call the roll of all the Elizabethan chroniclers, most of whom accepted Geoffrey of Monmouth at his face value. Among Spenser's later contemporaries John Speed was even more skeptical than the "learned and vnpartiall" Camden,[189] and in his contributions to Michael Drayton's *Poly-Olbion* (1613) John Selden wrote his skepticism without equivocation:

> The Author, in Passages of *first Inhabitants, Name, State*, and *Monarchique succession* in this Isle, followes *Geffrey* ap *Arthur, Polychronicon, Matthew* of *Westminster*, and such more. Of their Traditions, for that one so much controuerted, and by *Cambro-Britons* still maintayned, touching the *Troian-Brute*, I haue (but as an Aduocat for the Muse) argued; disclaiming in it, if alledg'd for my own Opinion.[190]

Such beliefs to Selden were like many other bits of floating tradition, "euen equally warrantable, as *Ariosto's* Narrations of Persons and Places in his *Rowlands, Spensers* Elfin Story, or *Rablais* his strange discoueries."[191]

As to Spenser's own critical attitude toward the ancient British history we can merely speculate. Perhaps his point of view was like that of Irenæus in *A Veue of the Present State of Ireland*. Irenæus dismisses the story of Brutus as a "vaine tale" by drawing a parallel with the story of Gathelus the

Spaniard, in the belief of which the Irish do "no otherwise, then our vaine English-men doe in the Tale of Brutus, whom they devise to have first conquered and inhabited this land, it being as impossible to proove, that there was ever any such Brutus of Albion or England, as it is, that there was any such Gathelus of Spaine." [192] But he refers in the same speech to Kings Arthur and Gurgunt even as he refers later to Kings Egfrid and Edgar, asserting that both Gurgunt and Arthur once had Ireland under their sway.[193] In the *De Rebus Gestis Britanniae Commentarioli Tres* by one E. S., whom Frederic I. Carpenter would take to be Spenser himself,[194] Brutus and Arthur are treated as historical figures, and recognition is made of the alignment of English writers against Polydore Vergil. The chronicler sees himself in the historical field even as Bacon saw himself in the sphere of science:

Non vt perficerem, aut illustrarem ipse, sed vt aliorum excitarem studia, qui id optimè facere possunt, informaui. Dolendum enim est historiam hanc, quae tot, tantas, & tàm praeclaras res contineat, ita iacere. Nam cùm non ferenda Anglicanorum turba scriptorum videatur, tùm nescio quid in Polidoro desidero.[195]

Carpenter assigns the chronicle conjecturally to the year 1582, and concludes that "Spenser's skepticism was very probably a development of later date." [196]

But be Spenser's attitude toward the ancient British history what it may have been, early or late in life, the poet needs no advocate for his muse. Nor does Sidney, who, despite his appeasing Lhuyd's ghost with a hearty laugh, "had ane intention to have transformd all his Arcadia to the stories of King Arthure." [197] We should certainly not expect Spenser's own critical views to have been so partisan as those of the fanatical Lhuyd or Richard Harvey, who considered the "Britons" superior to the other members of the growing British empire. Spenser, like Hakluyt, may have considered Geoffrey's *Historia* essentially a "historie of the Kings of England," but it does not necessarily follow that he, like Richard Harvey, subscribed to all "the markes and circuites, that *Geffry Monmouth* hath set downe." Rather, we should expect Spenser to have reacted, if not like Speed and Selden, then more like Camden, whom he pauses in *The Ruines of Time* to praise as the "nourice of antiquitie." [198] Spenser's use of Brutus and Arthur does not imply credulity so much as it implies a thorough knowledge of the literary pabulum of his age. From 1544 to 1615, from Leland to Howes, through Spenser's school days, through the composition and publication of *The Faerie Queene*, to the time of Spenser's death, Geoffrey of Monmouth was considered by Welsh-

men and by most Englishmen as the champion of
the growing empire of Great Britain, and the controversy that accordingly raged over the historicity of Brutus and Arthur could not have been
disregarded by a poet of Spenser's antiquarian pre-
dilections. Without the elder tradition of "the
Ynys Brydain that Geoffrey rescued from oblivion
. . . . there would have been a poorer Spenser." [199]
Without the interpretation put upon Geoffrey by
Spenser's contemporaries, there would not have
been a better Spenser. Leland, Kelton, Bale, John
Caius, Lhuyd, Sir John Price, Richard Price, Lambard, Powel, Churchyard, Richard Harvey, Sir
Henry Savile, Stow, Howes — an imposing array:
and they were not without reserves, named and
unnamed, who, at one time or another, helped them
to raise the Old Harry and sacrifice upon the altar of
patriotism Polydore Vergil, William of Newburgh,
Gildas, Boccaccio, Hector Boece, George Buchanan, Vives, Jean Bodin, John of Whethamstede,
Hadrian Junius, and others. And be it observed
that Geoffrey was defended, and Polydore and his
"complices" condemned, in verse as well as in
prose.

Except for the support of the Catholic contro-
versialist Thomas Stapleton, Polydore apparently
won little commendation until the turn of the century, and then from the feudal Sir Thomas Craig,

who, in *Scotland's Soveraignty Asserted* (*ca.* 1603),
takes the typical Scottish attitude toward the story
of Arthur. As much abuse as the English and
Welsh had heaped on Polydore for cavilling at
Geoffrey, Sir Thomas, in return, scatters on them
for cavilling at Polydore. To Sir Thomas, Polydore is first "a most Learned English Historian"
and then "the only Man that hath writ the History
of *England* with Judgment": [200] "*Polydore Virgil*
endeavoured to rid his History of those Milesian
Tales, and old Wives Fables, but he durst not
openly detract from them, though he does mani-
festly distinguish his History from that new one of
the Babler *Geffrey* of *Monmouth*; yet we see he is in
no Esteem amongst the English, though he be their
only Historian, who has writ with any Judgment." [201] From these words and from those that
follow there can be no doubt concerning the weight
of public opinion about Arthur in Spenser's day:
"*Polidore* does plainly say, that this *Arthur* died in
the very flower of his Youth; being afraid of the
Indignation of the Vulgar, if he had writ nothing
of him." [202]

One word more: for the Elizabethans would not
let Polydore's bones rest in peace. Not only did
Polydore write against the venerable tradition of
Geoffrey of Monmouth, but also, according to the
report of John Foxe, John Caius, and other gos-

sipers, he burned his very sources and shipped valuable English manuscripts off to Italy. Polydore was therefore goaded by his tormentors on several counts, and there was not even one to appease his ghost with a hearty laugh as Sidney had appeased Lhuyd's. It is well enough that the following invective is anonymous:

Polydorus Vergilius, — that most rascall dogge knave of the worlde, an Englishe man by byrth, but he had Italian parents: he had the randsackinge of all the Englishe lybraryes, and when he had extracted what he pleased he burnt those famous velome manuscripts, and made himself father to other men's workes — felony in the highest degree; he deserved not heaven, for that was to good for him, neither will I be so uncharitable as to judge him to hell, yet I thinke that he deserved to be hanged between both.[203]

One thing is sure: when Ponsonby was publishing *The Faerie Queene*, the Arthurian wing of the Ancients was in triumph over the Moderns, and without sweetness and light.

That the opponents of Geoffrey of Monmouth in Spenser's day found themselves thoroughly "welshed" is obvious, and this picture of Spenser's Arthurian setting would not be complete without some notice of the comic Welshman as he appears in Tudor England. Let Lhuyd himself, in his patriotic seriousness, give the earlier glimpse. Lhuyd holds that the prestige of Wales had crossed

ouer the Riuer *Dee*, cheifly since the beginnyng of the
reigne of *Henry the seuenth*, a moste prudent Prince:
vntill this day. Who, lineally descēdyng from his grandfather, *Owen Tudyr*, a *welshman*, borne in the Ile of
Anglysey: quite deliuered all the *welshmen* from such
lawes of bondage, as in other kynges dayes they were
subiect vnto. And the most mightie Prince, kynge
Henry the eight, his sonne: deliuered them wholy from
all seruitude, and made them in all poyncts equall to the
Englishmen. Whereby it commeth to passe, that laying
aside their old manners, they, who before were wonte to
liue most sparingly: are now enritched and do imitate
the *Englishmen* in diet, & apparell, howbeit, they be
somedeale impatient of labour, and ouermuch boastyng
of the Nobilitie of their stocke, applying them selues
rather to the seruice of noble men, then geuynge them
selues to the learnyng of handycraftes. So that you shall
finde but few noble men in *England*, but that the
greater parte of their retinew (wherin *Englishmen* ex-
ceede al other nations) are *welsh men* borne. For men
cheifly brought vp with Milke meates, beyng nymble,
and well set of bodie: are very apt to do any kynde of
businesse. Besides, beyng somwhat high minded, and
in extreame pouertie, acknowledgyng the nobilitie of
their famely: are more giuen to the culture, and trim-
myng of their bodies (like *Spayniards*) then to ritches,
or the belly, and beynge very apt to learne courtlike
behauiour: are therfore by the English nobilitie, preferred before Englishmen.[204]

But even Lhuyd, extremist though he is, is fair
enough to state that in the matter of pedigrees the
Welsh "are too too curious," and he continues:
"They thinke as well of them selues, as either the

Frenchmen, the Turkes, or Latines, deriuing their originall from the *Troians*."[205]

Information about certain pastimes in North Wales about the year 1575 shows how seriously the Elizabethan Welshman took his ancestry and his stories of Arthur:

Upon the Sundays and Holidays the multitude of all sorts of men, women, and children of every parish do use to meet in sundry places, either on some hill or on the side of some mountain where their Harpers and Crowthers sing them songs of the doings of their Ancestors; namely of their wars against the Kings of this realme, and the English nation; and then do they rip up their pedigrees at length, how each of them is descended from their old Princes. Here also do they spend their time in hearing some part of the lives of Thalaassyn, Marlin, Beno, Rybbye, Jermin, and such other the intended Prophets and Saints of that country.[206]

In the seventeenth century Martin Parker poked fun at "two undaunted Troian worthies," mighty "branches of *Cadwalader*":

> For surely tis a rare example,
>   Who now will feare to fight with ten,
>   When these two lads (with courage ample)
> Opposed fifteene thousand men,
>   Then heigh for *Wales*,
>   *Scots* strike your Sayles,
>   For all your proiects nought prevailes,
>   True *Brittains* scorne to turne their tayles.[207]

And as late as the eighteenth century a playful rimester could still get a tune from the old strings:

And merry Harpers waste their Days
In *Druid*'s Songs, and *British* Lays,
'Till they get drunk, and make a Pudder
About their Hero *Owen Tudor*;
And, like *Cadators*, disagree
Concerning Genealogy.[208]

But in Spenser's day the magic pen of Shakspere
is more to point, and not to dilate upon Sir Hugh
Evans, the Welsh parson, or upon Owen Tudor's
cousin, Owen Glendower — who was versed in the
skimble-skamble of "the dreamer Merlin and his
prophecies" and who convinced Hotspur that
even "the devil understands Welsh " — Shakspere's glorification of Captain Fluellen in the field
before Harfleur and at Agincourt is sufficient.
Fluellen moves about in the immortal company of
Pistol and Captains Jamy, Macmorris, and Gower,
and he carries away the honors for Wales.

When Harry of Monmouth agrees with Fluellen
that "Edward the Plack Prince of Wales, . . .
fought a most prave pattle here in France," the
following conversation ensues between Harry and
Fluellen:

Flu. If your Majesties is rememb'red of it, the Welshmen did good service in a garden where leeks did grow,
wearing leeks in their Monmouth caps; which, your
Majesty know, to this hour is an honourable badge of
the service; and I do believe your Majesty takes no scorn
to wear the leek upon Saint Tavy's day.

K. Hen. I wear it for a memorable honour; For I am Welsh, you know, good countryman.

Flu. All the water in Wye cannot wash your Majesty's Welsh plood out of your pody, I can tell you that. Got pless it and preserve it, as long as it pleases His grace, and His majesty too! . . . . By Jeshu, I am your Majesty's countryman, I care not who know it. I will confess it to all the 'orld. I need not to be ashamed of your Majesty, praised be God, so long as your Majesty is an honest man.

King Henry was no doubt amused, but it was his sober judgment that

> Though it appear a little out of fashion,
> There is much care and valour in this Welshman.

Pistol, however, reckons otherwise with Fluellen's valor, but the "base Troyan" teaches him at length the inadvisability of mocking at leeks upon Saint Davy's Day. "Not for Cadwallader and all his goats," swears Pistol, would he eat the leek, but he does eat it, and he eats it sauced. Pistol takes the groat to heal his pate, too, in lieu of another leek in reserve in Fluellen's pocket, and he and his "ploody coxcomb" are waved farewell with the words of Captain Gower:

Will you mock at an ancient tradition, begun upon an honourable respect, and worn as a memorable trophy of predeceased valour, and dare not avouch in your deeds any of your words? I have seen you gleeking and galling at this gentleman twice or thrice. You thought, because he could not speak English in the native garb, he could not therefore handle an English cudgel. You find it otherwise; and henceforth let a Welsh correction teach you a good English condition.[209]

A Welsh correction for an English condition — Captain Gower is quite right, for Shakspere's portrayal of Fluellen has an additional significance in the fact that Fluellen is as English as he is Welsh. He and Captains Jamy, Macmorris, and Gower represent Wales, Scotland, Ireland, and England, but at the same time they represent a sort of United States of Great Britain. Fluellen's Welsh dispute with the Irish Macmorris is forgotten in the midst of English bravery at Agincourt. King Henry himself is Welsh, but he is English as well, and he is a national hero. When he gives the battle-cry of "God for Harry! England and Saint George!" he is but sounding the call for more English soldiers like John Bates, Alexander Court, and Michael Williams, captained by such an officer as Gower — "Rotarian" Englishmen, if you please, as illustrated by the satire of Beaumont and Fletcher's *Knight of the Burning Pestle*.[210]

The customary interpretation of *The Knight of the Burning Pestle* is that it is a satire mainly on a type of play, founded upon chivalric romance, which was popular at that time among the tradespeople of London. But it is also a satire on contemporary patriotism, really an exaggerated form of primitivism, which, especially from the time of Henry VII, had sifted down from the court and the nobility into the life of the streets. "I doe not call to minde," says Ralph, "that I yet read of a Grocer Errant, I will be the said Knight."[211] And when Ralph, "an English man, As true as steele, a hearty Englishman,"[212] harangues his soldiers at Mile End in the name of Saint George, he is but exemplifying Harry of Monmouth's speech before Harfleur: "Is not all the world Mile-end, Mother?" "No *Michael*, not al the world boy, but I can assure thee *Michael*, Mile-end is a goodly matter."[213]

A mustering of soldiers or a display of archery at Mile End no doubt furnished a gay outing for the families of grocers, merchant tailors, leather-sellers, and in this connection Prince Arthur's London Knights of the Round Table become a part of the psychology of the "one hundred per cent" Englishman. A ludicrous slant is thereby given to the organization, even as the typical Welshman made himself ludicrous by forever doting on genealogy or leeks or the kinship of Saint David and Arthur or the authenticity of Geoffrey of Monmouth. Thus Thomas Smith, "customer" Prince Arthur; Hugh Offley, sheriff Sir Lancelot; Richard Robinson, leather-seller poet laureate, are not far removed in spirit from Ralph, Knight of the Burning Pestle and model grocer's apprentice, who refuses the King of Moldavia's daughter for black-thumbed Susan, cobbler's maid in Milk Street: "There's properer women in London then any are there I-wis." [214]

But if the Tudor interest in the Arthurian legend is a part of a primitivistic movement which has its ludicrous side, nevertheless this absurdity comes not from the fact that there was a revival of interest in the Arthurian legend. The revival itself was essentially noble. The absurdity comes, on the other hand, from the interest of the tradespeople, who appear in as ridiculous a light as Don Quixote of la Mancha.[215] From this point of view there is no inconsistency in Spenser, nor would he have violated his own high principles by becoming enthusiastic, say, over such an organization as Prince Arthur's London Round Table, in whose society the Arthurian knights of Edward III would have felt sadly out of place. Considered historically, from the very first prophecies of Arthur's return, as a sort of epic tradition, the Arthurian right of English kings becomes a national matter of serious import. There is no better example of this seriousness in Spenser's age than Leicester's famous entertainment for Elizabeth at Kenilworth in 1575, where the chief nobility of England assembled for twelve festal days. The letter of Robert Laneham,

"Mercer" and "freend officer attendant in the Coourt, vnto hiz fréend a Citizen, and Merchaunt of London," Humphrey Martin, gives a running story of the festivities.[216] *The Princelye pleasures, at the Courte at Kenelwoorth* (1576),[217] the account left by George Gascoigne, master of revels for the occasion, gives the literary programme, and reveals better just how the entertainment was shot through with the Arthurian legend. When Elizabeth entered the first gate of the castle grounds, six trumpeters "hugelie advaunced," signifying "that in the daies and Reigne of K. *Arthure*, mē were of that stature. So that yᵉ Castle of *Kenelworth* should seeme stil to be kept by *Arthurs* heires and their servants." [218] It is true that "Zabeta" departed very suddenly,[219] but she was irritated because she had a crow to pick with Leicester, not because her Welsh blood may have been connected with Arthur of Britain. That the Arthurian legend reached down also into Mile End Green, therefore, does not compromise the seriousness of the theme, just as Spenser's nobility is not compromised by any interest he may have had in such a democratic extension of an aristocratic tradition. From the point of view of Renaissance theories of poetry, Spenser's use of the Arthurian legend is founded upon the rocks of Parnassus.

CHAPTER IV

LITERARY CRITICISM

Or els (whiche wer muche) proue him to be
Arthur himself.

THOMAS WILSON,
The Arte of Rhetorique, 1553.

For a Heroik poeme, he said, ther was no such
ground as King Arthurs fiction.

BEN JONSON, according to Drummond
of Hawthornden.

FOR understanding Spenser's use of the Arthurian legend from the point of view of literary
criticism, the tenets characteristic of Renaissance
theories of poetry that are most important in-
volve mainly the concept of the "learned poet," the
concept of the epic as the chief of the "kinds" of
poetry, and the concept of decorum. "The Matter
of Britain," writes Professor Renwick, "was inevitable to Spenser, and it could be defended upon
the best classical precedents." [1] But Professor
Renwick is not primarily concerned with Spenser's
use of the Arthurian legend, and he omits, without
disturbing the equilibrium of his thesis, some con-
necting links which are significant for our study.

The idea of the "learned poet," which was as old
as Horace's *Ars Poetica,* can best be illustrated in

its relation to Spenser by resorting to the Italian Giovanni Battista Giraldi Cinthio, the Frenchman Joachim Du Bellay, and Gabriel Harvey, Spenser's friend at Pembroke College. In his *Discorsi dei Romanzi* (Venice, 1554), Giraldi Cinthio gives advice to the young scholar-poet:

Gioua anco al compositore, parlar con gli artefici di quell'arti, delle quali egli è per trattare, come co medici della salute de i corpi, & della qualità delle membra, & della loro natura, co sauij delle consulte, co gli Astrologhi del cielo, co Cosmographi della terra & del mare, & de fiumi & de uiaggi, co naturali de i principij delle cose & della lor generatione, co marinari dell'arte del nauicare, co capitani delle guerre, delle ordinanze, & de fatti d'arme, co caualieri de corsieri & delle giostre, co principi del reggere i popoli, & le città.[2]

Du Bellay, in setting down the qualifications of an epic poet in *La Deffence et Illustration de la Langue Francoyse* (1549), states that he should be, among other things, "instruict de tous bons ars et sciences, principalement naturelles et mathematiques."[3] Gabriel Harvey himself speaks words of wisdom indicative of the fruits of the New Learning:

Other commend Chawcer, & Lidgate for their witt, pleasant veine, varietie of poetical discourse, & all humanitie: I specially note their Astronomie, philosophie, & other parts of profound or cunning art. . . . It is not sufficient for poets, to be superficial humanists: but they must be exquisite artists, & curious vniuersal schollers.[4]

According to Harvey, Spenser shared some of his views: "M. Spenser conceiues the like pleasure in the fourth day of the first Weeke of Bartas. Which he esteemes as the proper profession of Urania." [5] And again, "Pudet ipsum Spenserum, etsi Sphaerae, astrolabijque non planè ignarum; suae in astronomicis Canonibus, tabulis, instrumentisque imperitiae." [6]   This same Harvey would find that information in

> All kinde of bookes, good and badd,
> Sayntish and divelish, that are to be hadd.
> Owlde and yunge,
> For matter and tunge,
> Wheresoever they dwell,
> In heaven or in hell;
> Machiavell, Aretine, and whome you will,
> That ar any waye renownid for extraordinary skill;
> Ether with myne owne familiar aloane,
> Or when twoe of us, like dogges, strive for a boane.[7]

In his dissatisfaction with "Italish Inglande," Harvey also seems to share Spenser's yearning for an idealized past when knighthood was in flower:

> Where owld Inglande?   Where owld Inglish
>   fortitude and might?
> Oh, we ar owte of the way, that Theseus,
>   Hercules, Arthur,
> And many a worthy British knight were woonte
>   to triumphe in.[8]

Although Spenser could not indorse Harvey's views about classical metres, nevertheless the words of Irenæus in *A Veue of the Present State of*

Ireland show that Harvey's stress on learning was
not a bad influence for a young poet, and they
show, furthermore, that the wave of antiquarianism in Tudor England had reached Spenser with
telling effect:

> But I doe herein relye upon those bardes or Irishe
> Cronicles, though the Irishe themselves, through their
> ignorance in matters of learninge and deepe judgement,
> doe most constantly beleve and avouch them. But unto
> them besides I adde my owne readinge; and out of them
> both togeather, with comparison of tymes, likenes of
> manners and customes, affinitie of words and names,
> properties of natures and uses, resemblances of rights
> and ceremonies, monuments of Churches and Tombes,
> and many other like circumstances, I doe gather a
> likelyhood of truth; not certenly affirminge any thinge,
> but by conferringe of tymes, language, monuments, and
> such like, I doe hunte out a probabilitie of thinges,
> which I leave unto your judgement to beleve or refuse.[9]

David Powel's account of his preparations for
compiling *The historie of Cambria* (1584), which he
composed at the request of Sir Henry Sidney and
which he dedicated to Sir Philip, is typical of the
antiquarian fervor of Spenser's age, and is similar
to the experience of Irenæus:

> Againe, I got all the authors that I could come by,
> which haue anie thing written of the affaires of VVales,
> as Gildas, Asser Meneuensis, Galfride, William of New-
> borow, Matthew Paris, Matthew Westminster, Thomas
> Walsingham, Ponticus Virunnius, Polydor Virgil, Io.

Leyland, Io. Bale, I. Prise, Matthew Parker, Io. Caius,
VVilliam Lambert, and all the English Chronicles
printed. In written hand I had Gildas Sapiens *alias*
Nennius, Henrie Huntington, VVilliam Malmsbury,
Marianus Scotus, Ralph Cogshall, Io. Euersden, Nicholas Triuet, Florentius Vigorniensis, Simon of Durham,
Roger Houedon, and other which remaine in the cus-
todie of I. Stowe citizen of London, who deserueth
cōmendation for getting togither the ancient writers of
the histories of this land. I had also Brytish books of
petegrees. I. Castoreus, & Syluester Giral. Cambrensis,
which with diuers other rare monuments of antiquitie,
I receiued at the hands of the Right Honorable the Lord
Burghley high treasurer of England: who also directed
me by his letters to all the offices where the Records of
this realme are kept, out of the which I haue gathered a
great part of this historie, and more would haue done, if
the time had permitted.[10]

Spenser's manifold interests — geography, topography, ancient national customs, linguistics,
and the like — throughout *A Veue of the Present
State of Ireland* reveal his varied antiquarian tastes,
and may well indicate that he intended to build in
his masterpiece a *speculum* of the knowledge of
Elizabethan England.[11] If more evidence is necessary than the very inclusiveness of *The Faerie
Queene* itself, Spenser's little known poem *The
Teares of the Muses* is enough to insure him a gram-
marian's funeral. "Nihil magis pudendum, quàm
ignarum esse suae Patriae,"[12] wrote Harvey at the
end of his own copy of *The Breuiary of Britayne*

(1573) — the very tract in which Lhuyd had poured gall on Polydore Vergil and Hector Boece for doubting the historicity of Brutus and Arthur. We may rest assured, therefore, that Spenser considered the Arthurian legend a heritage of his native land and an integral necessity for the learning of an epic poet. He "was the poet of the antiquarianism of sixteenth-century England, as Parker was its patron and Camden its most active worker."[13] It is significant that Eudoxus, in *A Veue of the Present State of Ireland*, was charmed by the learning of Irenæus: "This rippinge up of Auncestries, is very pleasinge unto me, and indeed savoreth of good conceiptes, and some reading withall."[14]

The idea of the Renaissance critics that the epic is the chief of the "kinds" of poetry was modified by a confusion with romance. Among the French critics the distinction between the nature of epic and romance seems not to have occurred. Du Bellay heads his chapter on the subject simply "Du long poëme francoys."[15] Like Ariosto, he exhorts,

Comme luy donq', qui a bien voulu emprunter de nostre langue les noms et l'hystoire de son poëme, choysi moy quelque un de ces beaux vieulx romans francoys, comme un *Lancelot*, un *Tristan*, ou autres: et en fay renaitre au monde un admirable *Iliade* et laborieuse *Eneïde*.[16]

Pierre de Ronsard thought the body of the *Orlando Furioso* "misshapen and monstrous,"[17] yet he introduced his coldly classical *Franciade* (1572) with the following words:

Je dy cecy pource que la meilleure partie des nostres pense que la *Franciade* soit une histoire des rois de France, comme si j'avois entrepris d'estre historiographe, et non poëte; bref, ce livre est un roman comme l'*Iliade* et l'*Aenëide*, où par occasion, le plus brefvement que je puis, je traitte de nos princes, d'autant que mon but est d'escrire les faits de Francion, et non de fil en fil, comme les historiens, les gestes de nos rois.[18]

In the second preface to *La Franciade* (1587), where he states that he has followed Homer, Ronsard adds that the good poet Homer, indeed, "fondé sur quelque vieil conte de son temps de la belle Heleine et de l'armée des Grecs à Troye, comme nous faisons des contes de Lancelot, de Tristan, de Gauvin et d'Artus, fonda là dessus son Iliade."[19]

Among the Italian critics an attempt was made to differentiate epic and romance, although whereever possible Ariostan romance and Vergilian epic were identified. Giraldi Cinthio makes the following attempt to explain the differences:

I soggetti, o le materie di i Romanzi non sono di quella maniera, che sono quelle di Vergilio, et di Homero. Perche l'uno et l'altro di questi nelle sue cõpositioni si ha preso ad imitare una sola attione di un'huomo solo, & i

nostri ne hanno imitate molte, non solo di uno, ma di
molti. Perche soura otto o dieci persone fondano tutta
la fabrica del loro cōponimēto.[20]

Giovanni Battista Pigna, in *I Romanzi* (Venice,
1554), brings the structure of romance closer to
that of epic:

Questa illustre attione à essere Epica, farà vna sola
d'una sola persona. . . . I Romanzi si dan bene à piu
fatti di piu huomini, ma che vn huomo specialmente si
propongono: il quale sia soura tutti gli altri celebrato.
& cosi con gli Epici concorrono nel pigliare vna sola
persona. ma nel prendere vn sol fatto non è cosi:
percioche tanti ne trattano, quanto lor pare essere
assai.[21]

But their "final position," according to Professor
Renwick, "was much like that of Dryden in regard
to Shakespeare: this was not the form as Aristotle
had defined it, but it had so much in common, and
was so undeniably good of its kind, that had Aristotle known it he might have extended his defini-
tion to include it."[22]

Spenser's conception of himself as an epic poet,
therefore, as a follower of Vergil, the "Romish
Tityrus," who

eft did sing of warres and deadly drede,[23]

did not conflict with his conception of *The Faerie
Queene* as a romance of chivalry on the pattern of
the *Orlando Furioso*.[24] In the October eclogue of

The Shepheardes Calender, Piers thus encourages Cuddie, who is despairing of his pastorals:

> Abandon then the base and viler clowne,
> Lyft vp thy selfe out of the lowly dust:
> And sing of bloody Mars, of wars, of giusts,
> Turn thee to those, that weld the awful crowne.
> To doubted Knights, whose woundlesse armour rusts,
> And helmes vnbruzed wexen dayly browne.
>
> There may thy Muse display her fluttryng wing,
> And stretch herselfe at large from East to West:
> Whither thou list in fayre *Elisa* rest,
> Or if thee please in bigger notes to sing,
> Aduaunce the worthy whome shee loueth best,
> That first the white beare to the stake did bring.[25]

E. K.'s gloss refers both to "Heroicall argument" and to "mater of knighthoode and cheualrie."[26] In a letter to Spenser (May, 1580), Harvey says that Spenser "flatly professed" in one of his "last Letters" to "ouergo" the *Orlando Furioso* in *The Faerie Queene*.[27]

Spenser's subsequent plan to combine both the alternatives offered by Piers to Cuddie and the alternatives offered by E. K.'s gloss seemed quite harmonious to him. The Arthurian legend was to Spenser epic in scope, but the bulk of its substance reached him in the form of romance. In the mere selection of the legend of Arthur, a national storehouse, Spenser was following the epic precedents of Homer, Vergil, and Ronsard; in the use of Arthurian romance, and in the choice to invent the

majority of his knights and ladies and to portray
the adventures of Arthur before he became king, he
was following the romance precedents of Boiardo,
Ariosto, and Tasso. Indeed, Spenser's host of new
acquaintances for Arthur was justified by the very
nature of romance itself and by Pigna, who writes:
"Artù Re d'Inghilterra vna corte hauea che non so-
lamente di paesani nell'arme valorosi fioriua; ma
di cauallieri etiandio d'altre regioni."[28] Spenser
combines the form of epic and romance by having
both books and cantos, but he differs from Ariosto's
example of *canti* by grouping the cantos together
by twelves to gain an additional form of epic
unity.[29] Professor Renwick says that "the coinci-
dence of the Twelve Paladins and the Twelve
Books of the Æneid probably had more to do with
the original plan of *The Faerie Queene* than any
'invention' or 'disposition' of the tale of Prince
Arthur."[30] But it is worth while to note that the
magic number *twelve* was connected with Arthur in
many ways. As early as Nennius, Arthur fought
twelve Herculean battles against the Saxons, and
this report, as against either Saxons or Saracens,
was Arthur's one achievement that caught the
imagination of the people. In Malory, Arthur
slays twelve kings, and the Grail romances frequently refer to twelve knights of the Round Table.
James Calfhill records in 1565 that Arthur "had

.xij. knightes of the rounde table," [31] and John Hardyng says that Galahad "made .xii. knightes of the order Of saynt Graall." [32] With Spenser's plan "to frame the other part of polliticke vertues" [33] in Prince Arthur's person in mind, it is interesting to observe that the number of knights whose names appear about the edge of the traditional Round Table at Winchester is twenty-four. Encircling the Tudor Double Rose in the centre is an inscription: "This is the rownde Table of Kyng Arthur with XXIIII. of his namyd Knyhtes." [34]

With the resultant romance-epic structure of *The Faerie Queene*, Spenser attempts to combine the single epic action of a single epic hero by interweaving Prince Arthur's search for Gloriana into the many actions of the many other knights and ladies. Consequently we should expect to find in *The Faerie Queene* the same sort of confusion as in the *Orlando Furioso* — a confusion of loose and casual story which resembles especially the Arthurian prose romances. [35] But thanks to the appearance of Tasso's *Gerusalemme Liberata* in 1580–81, Spenser was prompted to effect a more harmonious fusion of epic and romance elements than that achieved by Ariosto. [36] As Vergil glorified the *Gens Iulia* or Ariosto the House of Este or Ronsard the House of Valois, Spenser *overwent* them in glorifying the House of Tudor. [37] From the point of view of structure, *The Faerie Queene* lies happily somewhere near the *Æneid*, between the frigid *Franciade* and the overheated *Orlando Furioso*.

Spenser's desire to "emulate" or even "ouergo" Ariosto is thus made clearer by the rehearsal of critical dicta that the poet knew. The words in Harvey's letter of May, 1580, should be taken for what they say:

> To be plaine, I am voyde of al iudgement, if your *Nine Comœdies*, whervnto in imitation of *Herodotus*, you giue the names of the *Nine Muses*, (and in one mans fansie not vnworthily) come not neerer *Ariostoes Comœdies*, eyther for the finenesse of plausible Elocution, or the rarenesse of Poetical Inuention, than that *Eluish Queene* doth to his *Orlando Furioso*, which notwithstanding, you wil needes seeme to emulate, and hope to ouergo, as you flatly professed your self in one of your last Letters.[38]

Harvey misunderstood Spenser's use of "ouergo," as have many Spenser critics. "English Maro" and "English Homer" [39] may have earned the title of "English Ariosto" as well, but the Italianate title was not due to any slavish aping of the *Orlando Furioso*. Essex *overwent* Drake in singeing Philip's beard; Shakspere *overwent* Kyd in writing a tragedy of blood; Spenser *overwent* Ariosto in writing an epic of chivalry which glorified his sovereign on the basis of national legend.[40] Sidney had ventured to say: "I dare vndertake, *Orlando Furioso*,

or honest king *Arthur*, will neuer displease a Soul-
dier," [41] and Professor P. W. Long, who interprets
Harvey's words correctly, sees in Sidney's sentence
"a covert encouragement" for Spenser.[42] Ben Jonson, who was generally hostile to romances, assured Drummond of Hawthornden that "for a
Heroik poeme . . . ther was no such ground as
King Arthurs fiction." [43]

The final step in the evolution of the very stanza
which bears his name seems to have been suggested
to Spenser by an Arthurian poem. This poem,
which contains seven six-line stanzas riming
ababcc, was written by George Ferrers for Leicester's entertainment of Elizabeth at Kenilworth in
1575 and printed in George Gascoigne's account of
the revels. Gascoigne introduces it as follows:

When her Majestie was entred the gate, and come
into the base Court, there came unto her a Ladie attended with two Nimphes, who came all over the Poole,
being so conveyed, that it seemed shee had gone upon
the water. This Ladie named her selfe the Ladie of the
Lake, who spake to her Highnesse as followeth.[44]

Then come the seven stanzas of the typical elegiac
form, save that the last verse of each makes up the
significant alexandrine. The second and seventh
stanzas will be enough to quote:

> I am the Lady of this pleasant Lake,
>   who since the time of great king *Arthures* reigne
> That here with royal Court aboade did make,
>   have led a lowring life in restles paine.

Til now that this your third arrivall here
   doth cause me come abroad, and boldly thus appeare.

.   .   .   .

Wherefore I wil attend while you lodge here,
   (most peereles Queene) to Court to make resort,
And as my love to *Arthure* dyd appeere,
   so shalt to you in earnest and in sport,
Passe on Madame, you neede no longer stand,
   the Lake, the Lodge, the Lord, are yours for
      to cōmande.[45]

Miss Emma F. Pope notes these stanzas and quotes one, but, in fact, she proposes the various English elements which may have gone to make up Spenser's stanza only to reject them.[46] Professor Grierson and Mr. A. M. Clark call Miss Pope's objections "rather strained," and consider that Spenser's "alexandrine (which is like the kite's tail that steadies the whole) was perhaps suggested by one of the stanzas used by Ferrers."[47] Professor Greenlaw has ventured, regarding the entertainment: "Perhaps Spenser was present; he certainly knew about the pageant, and it might well have suggested some projects to him."[48] If Spenser heard the voice of the Lady of the Lake, surely he must have felt the striking effect of the final alexandrine. He uses precisely the form of Ferrers' stanza as the last stanza of the January eclogue of *The Shepheardes Calender*;[49] and even if Professor Greenlaw's "perhaps" must remain at the best only a plausible guess, yet there is no doubt that Spenser knew Gascoigne's account of the entertainment.[50] In respect to Spenser's use of the Arthurian legend, it is interesting to have even a tenable theory that from an Arthurian poem he learned the final step in the development of the Spenserian stanza, the postern of which he reckoned as important as the wicket or the keep.

The concept of decorum has chiefly to do with diction, but it also involves the use of allegory and the fusion of Arthurian romance with classical mythology. From Du Bellay, Spenser perhaps derived his greatest stimulus to plunder the classics and the romances for the enrichment of England's epic vocabulary. For all his *patrie*, Du Bellay disliked the Old French romances, yet he would permit "quelques motz antiques . . ., à l'example de Virgile": "Pour ce faire, te faudroit voir tous ces vieux romans et poëtes françoys."[51] In the second preface to *La Franciade* (1587), Ronsard speaks more pointedly:

Encore vaudroit-il mieux, comme un bon bourgeois ou citoyen, rechercher et faire un lexicon des vieils mots d'Artus, Lancelot et Gauvain, ou commenter le Romant de la Rose, que s'amuser à je ne sçay quelle grammaire latine qui a passé son temps.[52]

In the *Abbregé de l'Art Poetique François* (1565), he had been more cautious: "Tu ne rejetteras point les vieux mots de nos romans,"[53] but he adds that

the words should be selected prudently. However,
in deriving inspiration on this point from Du Bellay and Ronsard, Spenser turned their caution and
prudence into enthusiasm. His "dewe obseruing
of Decorum euerye where" had already been an
experiment in *The Shepheardes Calender* — a decorum, according to E. K., "in personages, in
seasons, in matter, in speach, and generally in
al seemely simplycitie of handeling his matter,
and framing his words." [54] Sidney, Daniel, and
Ben Jonson may have misunderstood the pastoral
Spenser, but King James VI of Scotland, in *Ane
Schort Treatise* (1585), recognized very well for
what purposes the poet could use "corruptit and
vplandis wordis." [55] The very antiquarian tastes of
Elizabethan England — an age, as Legouis says,
"of heated patriotism favourable to the revival
and glorification of all that pertained to the past of
Great Britain" [56] — were sufficiently palatable to
whet Spenser's appetite for the flavor of "prow,"
"persaunt," "belgardes," "beauperes," [57] and for
other "*waightie woords, vsde in King* Arthurs
daies." [58]

For the combination of classical and romantic
elements — even as "la Tauola rotonda" among
the Italians could be "come la Naue degli Argonau-
tici " [59] — if Spenser needed any other examples
than those afforded by Luigi Alamanni's Arthuriz-

ing of the *Iliad* in the *Avarchide* (1570),[60] and by
Tasso's far happier combination in *Gerusalemme
Liberata* (1580–81), he had a ready suggestion in
William Hunnis's device of the rescue of the Lady
of the Lake in Leicester's entertainment for Eliza-
beth at Kenilworth in 1575. Gascoigne obliges:

> *Tryton* in likenesse of a Mermaide, came towarde the
> Queenes Majestie as she passed over the bridge, return-
> ing from hunting. And to her declared that *Neptune*
> had sent him to hir highnes, to declare the wofull dis-
> tresse wherein the poore Ladie of the Lake did remaine,
> the cause whereof was this. Sir *Bruse*, *Sauns pittie*, in
> revenge of his cosen *Merlyne* the Prophet (whom for his
> inordinate lust she had inclosed in a rocke) did con-
> tinuallie pursue the Ladie of the Lake: and had (longe
> sithens) surprised hir, but that *Neptune* (pitying hir dis-
> tresse) had envyroned hir with waves. Whereupon she
> wasenforced to live alwaies in that Poole, and was therby
> called the Ladie of the Lake. Furthermore affirming
> that by *Merlynes* prophecie, it seemed she coulde never
> bee delivered but by the presence of a better maide
> then hir selfe. Wherefore Neptune had sent him right
> humbly to beseech hir majestie that she would no more
> but shew her selfe, and it should bee sufficient to make
> sir *Bruse* withdrawe his forces.[61]

Then follows the speech of Triton in verse, and
much more of the same nature. Professor W. E.
Mead comments on the episode: "Literal reproduction of the Arthurian legends was not aimed at,
for novelty was the chief feature of the whole entertainment."[62]

Spenser had ample precedent in Arthurian romance for the use of allegory. The idea of the moral significance of the epic was as old as Horace's *Epistolae*, and Giraldi Cinthio recognized the superiority of romance over epic for this purpose.[63] For the representation of his knights as embodying various virtues and portraying various types of men, Spenser could have known not only the multitudinous references to the virtues of the galaxy of knights surrounding "ARTHVRE the mirror of manhood and Champion of Cheualrie,"[64] but also the romances themselves which pictured Gawain as the flower of courtesy, or Lancelot as the prince of nobility, or (as in *Le Chevalier as deus espées*) Arthur as an ideal of social excellence. In the romances as well as in the classics, examples of virtues were employed to teach us what to do, and examples of vices to teach us what not to do. Just as Spenser selected from the classics, so he could select from the romances, and, like Sidney, and Milton later, he could absorb the spirit of both without compromising his conception of morality. Two of E. K.'s glosses to *The Shepheardes Calender*, in which he refers to "certain fine fablers and lowd lyers, such as were the Authors of King Arthure the great" and to the "packed pelfe and Massepenie religion" of "bald Friers and knauish shauelings,"[65] are in keeping with the humanistic revolt against the ro-

mances as a poor criterion of literary form and with
the post-Reformation objection to the romances as
the work of papists.[66] But if Spenser dictated, or
read and approved, E. K.'s remarks, it is but reasonable to follow Legouis and say that his "poetic
appetite for the beautiful and the picturesque had
the better of his reason."[67] Sidney himself affirmed: "Truely I haue knowen men, that euen
with reading *Amadis de Gaule*, (which God knoweth
wanteth much of a perfect Poesie) haue found their
harts mooued to the exercise of courtesie, liberali-
tie, and especially courage."[68] And despite Sidney's apology for *Amadis*, he nevertheless "had
ane intention," according to Ben Jonson, "to have
transformd all his Arcadia to the stories of King
Arthure."[69]

Spenser's use of political allegory was in a way
but a continuation of the mediæval *roman à clef*.
Professor J. M. Berdan, who would find Spenser's
precedents for allegory in his own English mediæval tradition,[70] says: "The author of the *Court
of Love* tried to impose it [*i. e.*, the allegorical poem
of the fifteenth century] intact upon the men of his
generation. And in spite of his undoubted genius,
he failed. Hawes, combining it with the chivalric
romance, produced a hybrid that pleased. Skelton
turned it to satire, and then contemptuously aban-
doned it altogether. And last of all Heywood

rather pathetically endeavored to support the
tottering structure by personalities and contemporaneous reference. And great was the fall
thereof. And yet, all these modifications are combined and assimilated by the genius of Spenser
into the *Faerie Queene*. There one finds the per-
sonified abstraction of the first, the chivalry of the
second, the satire of the third, and the historical
allusion, the episode of *Burbon* for example,[71] of
the fourth. . . . The many-sided genius of Spenser
took this medieval tradition, combined it with
humanism and with the Italian, — and the world
has forgotten the lesser men."[72]

But in connection with Spenser's use of the Arthurian legend, the world should not forget Thomas
Wilson, who in *The Arte of Rhetorique* talks directly
to Spenser. Under the heading of "Sport moued by
telling of old tales," Wilson writes:

IF there be any olde tale, or straunge historie, well
and wittelie applied to some man liuyng, all menne
loue to heare it of life. As if one were called Arthure
some good felowe that were wel acquainted with kyng
Arthures booke, and the knightes of his rounde table,
would want no matter to make good sport, and for a
nede would dubbe him knight of the rounde Table, or
els proue hym to be one of his kinne, or els (whiche wer
muche) proue him to be Arthur himself.[73]

Wilson's words, together with the bearing they
have on the living example of the contemporaneous existence of London's Prince Arthur and his

Knights of the Round Table, make the complete
identification. Prince Arthur or Artegal or Cali-
dore may not only be the symbols of the virtues of
"vn perfetto cauagliere"[74] or find their prototypes
at the court of Elizabeth, but with the authority of
Wilson they may also be, if Spenser wishes, actually the virtues and courtiers themselves. It is, in
fact, not supererogatory to hammer home once
more the significance of the contemporaneous existence of "the Worshipfull Societie of Archers, in
London yearely celebrating the renoumed memorie
of the Magnificent Prince ARTHVRE & his Knightly
Order of the Round Table."[75] London's "Magnificent" Prince Arthur may not be to the satisfac-
tion of all scholars "magnificence in particular . . .
according to Aristotle and the rest,"[76] yet he may
serve as an humble prototype for Robert Dudley,
Earl of Leicester, or for a composite picture of an
Elizabethan captain moving about Faeryland in
quest of Gloriana, England's Tudor Faery Queen.
Especially when much is made of Spenser's living
behind his age in the playground of mediæval
romance, it is of singular moment that even on one
occasion this "Magnificent" Prince and his
Knights while on their way to Mile End Green
"did their duty upon their knee" before Elizabeth
Tudor, and that she in return "most graciously
bowed her body."[77]

CHAPTER V

THE EARLY STUART PERIOD

Inglād and scotland sal be bot ane monarche, and sal lyue
vndir ane prince; and sa inglis men sal get there prophesie ful-
fillit to there auen mischeif.

> *The Complaynt of Scotlande, ca.* 1549.

Let vs be ashamed to bee last, or backward, seeing another
Arthur king of all great Brittaine raigneth.

> JOHN BRISTOLL, *The Ioiefull and Blessed Reuniting
> the two mighty & famous kingdomes, ca.* 1604.

REGARDLESS of the Scottish attitude toward
the Arthurian legend and the Welsh House of
Tudor, and regardless of James VI's attitude toward *The Faerie Queene*, the House of Stuart was
brought to the throne of England according to the
prophecy of Merlin as well as that of Thomas of
Erceldoune.[1] In his poem *To the Maiestie of King
Iames* (1603), Michael Drayton was quick to seize
upon the value of "*Tudors* blood," which

> As theyr great *Merlin* propheci'd before
> Should the old Brittons regalty restore,[2]

and the printed marginal commentary is "Owen
Tudor." Drayton continues:

> This Brittaine hope, *Iames* our vndoubted King,
> In true succession, as the first of other
> Of *Henries* line by Father, and by Mother.[3]

Drayton made no mention of Elizabeth, and James pretended to be shocked, reproved Drayton, and neglected him for the rest of his life. James did erect a noble monument to Elizabeth in Westminster Abbey, the only royal tomb on which are emblazoned the arms of Wales, but he did not love the Faery Queen who signed his mother's death warrant, and his irritation at Drayton may have been due in part to the Tudor connection insisted upon for him. In *A Souldiers VVish vnto His Soueraigne Lord King Iames* (1603), Robert Pricket sings in a strain similar to Drayton's when he exhorts "Englands people" to

> reioyce to see each princely bud,
> That springs from forth King *Henries* Royall bloud.[4]

At any rate, both prose-writers and other poets were not deterred from returning to the same theme.

No better example of the importance and seriousness of the king's descent in the minds of the people can be given than by citing the elaborate genealogy of James prepared by George Owen Harry, a Welsh parson. In 1604 Harry brought out his genealogy under the following flourish:

THE GENEALOGY OF THE HIGH AND MIGHTY *Monarch, Iames, by the grace of God, King* of great Brittayne, &c. with his lineall descent from *Noah, by diuers direct lynes to* Brutus, *first Inhabiter of* this Ile of Brittayne;

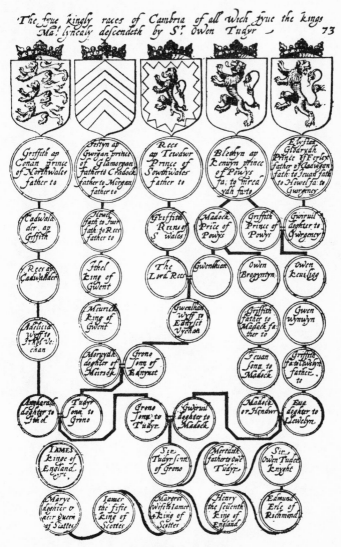

A Genealogy of James I in George Owen Harry's *Genealogy of
the High and Mighty Monarch, Iames*, 1604, Showing
the Descent of James from Owen Tudor.
(British Museum C.64.d.12.)

and from him to *Cadwalader*, the last King *of the Brittish bloud; and from thence, sundry wayes to his Maiesty*: wherein is playnly shewed his rightfull Title, by lawfull descent *from the said* Cadwalader, *as well to the Kingdome of Brittayne, as to* the Principalities of Northwales and Southwales: together with a *briefe Cronologie of the memorable Acts of the famous men touched in* this Genealogy, and what time they were. Where also is *handled the worthy descent of his Maiesties ancestour* Owen Tudyr, and his affinity with most of the greatest Princes of Christendome: *VVith many other matters worthy of note.*

In the text of Harry's treatise, the original of which is *The Wellspringe of true nobilitie* in manuscript,[5] James is pictured as "the second King of Brittayne, . . . bringing with him Vnity, Peace, and Profite to all these Realmes, by vniting and knitting together all the scattered members of the Brittish Monarchy, vnder the gouernment of him, as one sent of GOD, to fulfill his diuine predestinate will, reuealed to KADWALADER, as our ancient Histories doe testify, fifteene hundred yeeres past, that the time should come, that the Heires descended of his loynes, should be restored agayne to the Kingdome of BRITTAYNE, which was partly performed in King HENRY the seuenth; but now wholly fulfilled in his Maiesties owne person."[6] Welsh persistence would not be denied, and the importance of Owen Tudor is kept to the fore. In 1597 the "braue and gallant Gentleman" Owen had appeared with his spouse in Drayton's *Eng-*

lands Heroicall Epistles, and Owen had questioned
Catherine, in part:

> By our great *Merlin*, was it not fore-told,
> (Amongst his holy prophecies enrold)
> vvhen first he did of *Tudors* fame diuine,
> That Kings and Queenes should follow in our line?
> And that the Helme, (the *Tudors* auncient Crest)
> Should with the Flower-delice be drest;
> And that our Leeke, (our Countries chiefe renowne)
> Should grow with Roses, in the English Crowne? [7]

In Harry's genealogy, Owen's blood in Henry
VII, "the first Brittish King," [8] is made to flow
directly into the veins of Henry's daughter Margaret, the wife of James IV of Scotland; and thence
through James V to Mary Queen of Scots we arrive
at "her sonne Kinge *Iemie* . . . the onely and abso-
lute king of *Scotlande*," [9] the first of England of the
name and "the second King of Brittayne." Or, if
we prefer, since Henry VII was the great-grand-
father of both of James's parents, we may trace the
descent from Lady Margaret Douglas, the daughter of Margaret Tudor by her second husband,
Archibald Douglas, Earl of Angus, to Henry
Stuart, Lord Darnley, the son of Lady Margaret by
Matthew Stuart, Earl of Lenox. From the frieze
on the south side of the monument erected by
James to Elizabeth in Westminster Abbey, it appears that James himself preferred to trace his
Welsh descent through his father rather than

through his mother,[10] and this preference shows that he was interested in the blood of his Stuart grandfather, Matthew, Earl of Lenox. From the blood of this grandfather, indeed, James could trace his descent from Llewelyn ap Griffith, the last native Prince of Wales, and thus establish a British connection independent of the Welsh blood of his great-grandmother, Margaret Tudor.[11]

In *Poly-Olbion* (1613), which is dedicated to Prince Henry, Drayton, undeterred by James's rebuff, represents the various claims of royal descent. Sabrina in the Fifth Song reconciles the claims, and brings James to the English throne according to the prophecy of Merlin. Recognition is taken of the fact that in James, Welsh blood "doubly thrives,"[12] and in the spirit of the times Drayton might just as truthfully have written "trebly." James was indeed, by the grace of God, doubly King of England and "Great Britain"[13] — James, the "gracious King of second Troy."[14]

Prose tracts, chronicle history, and verse carry on the distinctly English point of view of tracing James's descent from Margaret Tudor. In *A Treatise of Vnion of the two Realmes of England and Scotland* (1604), one I. H. speaks of the union as follows: "King *Henry* the seuenth aimed at this Vnion, when he married his eldest daughter *Margaret* into *Scotland*. King *Henry* the eight and all

the chiefe Nobilitie of the realme expressely desired
it, when they laboured to haue a marriage knit be-
tweene *Edward* and *Mary*, the two young Princes
of both the kingdoms."[15] In the historical preface
to his edition of Stow's *Annales* (1615), Edmund
Howes states that, after the death of Elizabeth,
"the Crowne returned vnto the next and immediate heyre of *Henry* the Seauenth after the thrice
blessed and memorable coniunction of the houses
of *Yorke* and *Lancaster*, and king IAMES in all
loue and peace was triumphantly established."[16]
In *A Prophesie of Cadwallader, last king of the
Britaines* (1604), William Harbert of Glamorgan[17]
observes the continuation of Tudor blood and
mingles joy with sorrow. In Δαφνις Πολυστεφανος
(1605), Sir George Buck considers James

> Fortunes dearling, Pieties champion,
> Successor and heire in all by right
> To great King *Artur* Iesu's faithfull knight.[18]

He derives James from Owen Tudor, and heaps
complimentary epithets upon him: "sacred Sou-
eraign *IAMES*, . . . the true *Polystephanus*, the
Peace-maker, King *Arturs* successor, great *Ædgars*
heire, high *Seneschall* of *Albion*, the great *Briton*
&c."[19] To the long-winded John Thornborough,
Bishop of Bristol, with "another *Arthur* king of all
great Brittaine"[20] on the throne, it is immaterial

how the union was effected so long as the sovereign
is a Briton:

> In mine opinion, it is well observed in the Cronicle
> of Wales, how God was not pleased with the first change
> of the name of Brittaine into the name of England; for
> presently followed the terrible and cruel invasion of the
> *Danes*, & after that the conquest of the *Normans*. But
> memorable is it, that the Brittaines ruled al the whole
> Ile togither . . . even to the death of *Cadwallader*, the
> last King of Brittaines, and of the noble race of Troians.
> Which when in succeeding age many mightie & famous
> Kings of England, considered, they laboured by al
> meanes to recouer and resume the name and stile of
> Kings of great Brittaine, accounting it dishonorable,
> to leese any iot of the honor of there most princely
> progenitors. . . .
>
> Neither doe I esteeme the change of name, a matter of
> indifference, as if it were all one, whither we were called
> Brittaines, or cōtinued English, and Scottes. But in my
> Iudgement it is reason to alter all into Brittaines, be-
> cause it was our most ancient, and is the more honorable
> name.[21]

James is "likewise of *Henries* race" in "An excellent Song, made on the Successors of King *Henry*
the fourth. *To the Tune of* O man in desperation"
in Richard Johnson's *Crowne Garland of Golden
Roses* (1631).[22] At all events, the shade of Henry
VII should have been laid to rest, even if that of
England's Faery Queen was probably disturbed by
the fickleness of human nature and the penalties of
virginity.

Prince Henry and, in turn, Prince Charles were both created Prince of Wales — the first creations since that of Henry VIII as prince in 1503 and the last before that of George Augustus, afterwards George II, in 1714. Prince Henry is the last of the Nine Worthies, among whom are included Henry VII and Henry VIII, in Robert Fletcher's *Nine English Worthies* (1606). In Ben Jonson's *Speeches at Prince Henry's Barriers*, which was part of a celebration in honor of Prince Henry on January 6, 1610, James is represented as a monarch who

> Wise, temperate, just, and stout, claims Arthur's seat.[23]

Arthur appears as a star in the heavens and speaks to the Lady of the Lake:

> Nor let it trouble thy design, fair Dame,
> That I am present to it with my flame
> And influence; since the times are now devolv'd
> That Merlin's mystic prophecies are absolv'd,
> In Britain's name, the union of this Isle,
> And claim both of my sceptre and my style.[24]

Popular treatises rather vaguely link Charles I with Arthur. In William Slatyer's *Genethliacon. sive, Stemma Iacobi* (1630), both "Arthur K. of Bryt." and "Sir Owen Tudir K[t]" appear in the genealogy from God to Charles; and in Nicolas Hunt's *Newe Recreations* (1631), Arthur is the ninety-second king in a list of one hundred and forty-seven "English" kings from Brutus to

Charles.[25] An anagram declaring James "the successor of the valorous King *Arthur*" in John Phili-
pot's edition of Camden's *Remaines concerning
Britaine* (1637) reads as follows:

Charles Iames Steuart
CLAIMES ARTHVRS SEATE[26]

It is clear, then, that the Welsh extraction of the
English royal family through the accession of
Henry VII, with which was associated both the
Trojan and the Arthurian legend, was continued
as both an historical and a poetical tradition
through the earlier years of the Stuarts. But the
Stuarts were never received as Welsh with the enthusiasm that hailed the Tudors, and they lacked
the Tudor knack for feeling the pulse of the nation.
Accordingly, in the end the same fate awaited
Welsh genealogy that awaited both the fulfilled
and the unfulfilled prophecies of Merlin, of which
Mr. A. E. Parsons writes: "As the theory of Divine
Right faded and the belief in Parliamentary supremacy grew, the stories receded more and more
into the realm of poetical ornament and their influence on political thought disappeared.[27] They
survived, however, in poetical allusion and courtly
compliment until nearly the end of the Stuart
dynasty, but their sponsor was the Muse of History, not of Poetry, and when she finally disowned
them they passed into the limbo of forgotten

things."[28] Yet in addition to the religious, the constitutional, and the economic problems that resulted in the unpopularity of the Stuarts and cost Charles I his head, notice should also be given to the bell that Bacon rang to awaken a drowsy scientific spirit and to the sheer advancement of learning in the seventeenth century. The growth of inquiry and skepticism that produced a Bacon and a Bacon's *Historie of Henry the Seventh* tended also to bring Polydore Vergil into his own against Geoffrey of Monmouth, as is shown by the critical work of Degory Wheare and William Burton.[29] The prognostications of William Lilly, it is true, and of other Partridges of the same covey, continued to appeal to a certain type of mind, and the appeal was extended beyond the Commonwealth period. To Lilly's *VVorlds Catastrophe* (1647) Elias Ashmole contributed what proves to be the first English translation of the *Prophecies of Merlin*,[30] and in relating the prophecies to events of the reign of Charles I, Lilly observes that in interpreting "the last sixteen lines" Alanus de Insulis "failed exceedingly."[31] Ashmole's translation appears in Lilly's book under the following title:

A Prophecie of *Ambrose Merlin*, a Britaine, From the Translation of *Gefferey* of *Monmouth*: Ænigmatically therein delivering the Fate, and Period of the English Monarchy.

Lilly rather prolifically gave out other versions of
sundry "prophecies" of Merlin, and in *A Prophecy
of the W[h]ite King, wrote by Ambrose Merlin 900.
years since, concerning Charles the late King*
(1651),[32] he finds an explanation of the overthrow
of the Stuarts. The significance of the blood of
Margaret Tudor in the English royal family was
stressed as late as 1751, as is evidenced by the title-
page of the novel *The Life and Amours of Owen
Tideric Prince of Wales*,[33] which states that from
Owen "likewise are descended, by the eldest
Daughter of HENRY VII. the present ROYAL FAM-
ILY of GREAT BRITAIN, FRANCE, and IRELAND."
But the statement connotes nothing Arthurian,
and when we remark that the novel was "Printed
for WILLIAM OWEN," enough has been said. When
Arthurian prophecy was used to justify the down-
fall of English kings, then the Arthurian right of
English kings was no more.

It is not fanciful to see the influence of *The
Faerie Queene* in the verse and prose which praised
the Welsh blood of the Stuarts and linked them
with Arthur of Britain. Indeed, in *A Supplement
of the Faery Queene in three Bookes. Wherein are
allegorically described Affaires both military and
ciuill of these times,* verses left in manuscript
("finished Anno Dni. 1635") by Ralph Knevett,[34]
there is a continuation of Spenser's manner: "re-

nowned Charles" sits in "Arthurs seate," Henri-
etta Maria is styled Gloriana, and Prince Arthur
goes questing on in a Faeryland soon to be torn by
the clash of Roundhead and Cavalier.

In the preface to the *Supplement,* Knevett explains his purpose:

> This Romance [*i. e., The Faerie Queene* plus the *Sup-
> plement*] is grounded vpon the history of Arthur, King of
> the Britons, and scourge of the intrudeing Saxons. . . .
> In the person of this Prince, the Poet intended to por-
> traite the image of a braue Knight, perfected in the
> twelue morall vertues, which was to be comprised in
> twelue Bookes: also it was his intention (after the con-
> summation of this worke) to write another Booke of
> politicall vertues, and to describe in the person of
> Arthur, after hee came to bee a King the propertyes of
> a good Gouernour, and prudent Soueraigne: But this
> great Apelles preuented by death, or disaster, left his
> rare Venus vnfinished; for there bee onely sixe whole
> Bookes extant of this famous poeme, written by him-
> self.[35]

He then quotes from Spenser's letter to Ralegh,
beginning with Spenser's account of Prince Arthur's birth and education. Thereupon he thinks
"it meete to lend the curteous Reader a threed,
whereby hee may extricate himself out this Laby-
rinth" of the three books of the *Supplement*: "The
Seuenth Booke, of the Faery Queene containeing
the Legend of Albanio or Prudence," [36] "The
Eighth Booke of the Faery Queene containeing the
Legend of Callimachus or Fortitude," [37] and "The

Ninth Booke of the Faery Queene containeing the Legend of Sir Belcoeur or Liberalitye."[38] Three of the introductory stanzas to "The Seuenth Booke," or "the Legend of Albanio or Prudence," reveal significant praise of Charles I and his Queen:

1

(Most mighty Prince) who through thy prudence high,
　　This new borne westerne Empire mannagest,
　　Conserueing that most happy vnity,
　　Which thy Sires wisedome great, and fortune blest,
　　First planted in this fairest Ilands brest,
　　Thy most auspicious eyes daigne to reflect
　　Vpon this worke, in humble numbers drest:
　　Cheere vp my Muse, with thy serene aspect,
Whom first thy vertue mou'd this subiect to elect.

2

Thy soueraigne worth's the subiect of my Song:
　　Thou sitts't in Arthurs seate, and dost maintaine
　　The antique glory of the Britons strong:
　　Thou has't Astræa brought to earth againe,
　　The Golden Age reuiu'd is in thy raigne.
　　Vouchsafe this Legend meane to looke vpon,
　　Wherein as in a glasse thou may'st see plaine,
　　Those splendent vertues, which about thy throne
Are fix'd, like to a radiant Constellation.

3

(And thou Illustr'ous Queene) whose geniall Bed,
　　Sends forth such royall Babes, that Britaines Crowne,
　　The claymes of doubtfull heires, no more shall dread;
　　From thy Maiesticke Sphere, daigne to looke downe,
　　Vpon this Table, of thy high renowne:
　　Thou Gloriana ar't (oh Lady bright)
　　Whom British Arthur wonne (maugre the frowne
　　Of adverse Fate) in her are blazon'd right,
Thy beauty, bounty, and thy vertues exquisite.[39]

These few selections from the *Supplement* are vital in that they indicate somewhat of the interpretation put upon *The Faerie Queene* by Spenser's age and by the poet's immediate followers. They disclose a double influence: Knevett is moved not only by the Arthurian aspect of *The Faerie Queene*, but also by the historical and poetical tradition of the Arthurian right of English kings, which motivated *The Faerie Queene* in the height of Elizabeth's glory and continued to the reign of Charles I.

With hopes for the future, Knevett concludes the preface of "this Poeme, which is onely an exact treatise of Morall Philosophy, enveloped in an Allegoricall Romance":

> Three other morall vertues remaine to bee discoursed of (to make this Zodiacke perfect) Which if God shall giue me leaue to finish, I shall yet forbeare to write. . . . Vntill in the person of Arthur, after he came to bee a King, I haue framed the other part of politicke vertues, and consecrated the totall summe of my endeauours, to the immortall honour of my King, and countrey.[40]

But, like his master Spenser, Knevett failed to accomplish his design. A king's scaffold was already casting its shadow over Faeryland, and Prince Arthur wanders yet in a poet's dream. Samuel Sheppard missed a great opportunity to continue the tradition in *The Faerie King*:[41] he thought it "no shame to Jmmitate" Spenser, "great PRINCE OF POETS," but he chose to fashion his king in "an Heroicall Heliconian Dresse" rather than in Arthurian armor. Sheppard's Muse was not the Muse of Spenser: Oliver Cromwell was "King" of England.

CHAPTER VI

Conclusion

THE irrefragable evidence of the number of contributory influences shows conclusively that Spenser's journey to Camelot was not accidental, and it shows, furthermore, that Spenser could have seen clearly the major part of his vision before ever he sent England's Saint George and the Red Cross Knight pricking on the plain. Though he may have been grieved at the death of Sidney, and again at that of Leicester; though he was disappointed at the treatment meted out to him from the hands of the Queen he loved, and from the clenched fists of her prosaic Lord High Treasurer, there is no reason to believe that he later materially changed the plans that appealed to the poetic idealism of Piers in the October eclogue of *The Shepheardes Calender*. The rough ore of the chronicles and the Arthurian romances was his to draw upon for his fiction.[1] The previous literary handlers of various phases of the legend — John Lydgate, the unknown author of *Here begynneth a lytel treatyse of ÿ byrth & pphecye of Marlyn* (1510), William Hunnis, George Ferrers, George Gascoigne, Thomas Blenerhasset, William Warner,

Thomas Hughes, and others — all contributed little or nothing to Spenser, but they, like all "the rakehellye route of our ragged rymers," help to commend the Arthurian legend as the proper *materia poetica* and are essential for a complete understanding of the evolution of *The Faerie Queene*. An obscure work like Richard Lloyd's *Briefe discourse of the most renowned actes and right valiant conquests of those puisant Princes, called the Nine worthies* (1584), and scattered Arthurian allusions, which in themselves may count for naught, blend into the perfectly focussed picture. We may also believe that Spenser had his ear close to the ground of Arthurian tradition, for a poet who introduces "Sir *Douglas*" from *Chevy Chace* among the knights of Satyrane's tournament,[2] a poet who shows the myth-making faculty so conspicuously as Spenser, is not likely to have scorned ballads or any old wive's tale that may have contributed to his immediate creative fancy. Harvey's request in 1580 for "some odde fresh paulting threehalfepennie Pamphlet for newes: or some Balductum Tragicall Ballet in Ryme, and without Reason . . . or whatsoeuer else shall first take some of your braue London Eldertons in the Head,"[3] shows unquestionably that the poets' poet rubbed elbows with the crowd; and broadsides which sing, however haltingly, of King Arthur's "Noble Acts,"[4] which sing of a "Magnificent" Prince Arthur and his London Knights of the Round Table, which sing of a Tudor queen's Welsh descent, are in part emblematic of the temper of the crowd in which the young poet moved. Spenser's years of comparative exile in far-away Ireland, where the Faery King Dagda still held his court, served only to enhance the poet's romantic English vision. There was needed only the depth of his mediæval yearning and the breadth of his Renaissance imagination to transmute the vision into faery gold.

Henry Tudor's exile in Brittany, the "Little Britain" of the romances, afforded a happy parallel to Arthur in Avalon, and Lewis Glyn Cothi, in words eminently suggestive of Spenser's own chronicle history of victory and empire, had already brought the Briton Messiah from the hearth of Mona:

> A gwr o Wynedd a goronid;
>
> .   .   .   .   .   .
>
> O aelwyd Mon val y damunid
> Y cad y ddwylin sy 'n cyd ddilyd;
> O'r hen wreichionen penrhwymid pob dadl;
> Ar yr un anadl yr ennynid.[5]

And the man from North Wales was crowned; . . . . From the hearth of Mona, as was desired, were brought the two lines which are in common continuation; by the old spark every strife was muzzled in the same breath in which it was kindled.

John Leland, the nemesis of Polydore Vergil, had
extended and intensified the compliment:

> Optima spes rerum maestos solata Britaños
> Sorte reuicturum promisit, & omine laeto
> Arturum, obscuro lucem qui redderet orbi.
> Tempus adest.[6]

The time was indeed at hand, with the virgin
daughter of Henry VIII, "the last that remaineth
aliue of that lyne," [7] on the throne of England.
Patriotic John Dee, who in his own manuscript of
Geoffrey's *Historia* glossed "Aper . . . cornubiae"
with "Rex Arthur," [8] wrote as a final marginal
commentary on the *Historia* the following words:
"Annus iam primus et nonagesimus supra octin-
gentos agitur, ex quo Britannis regno expulsis
Saxonū gens rexq potiri coepit." [9] Patriotic Spenser, who saw the fulfilment of Merlin's prophecy in
"twise foure hundreth yeares," [10] turned his poetic
eyes towards Merionethshire, an ancestral seat of
the Penmynydd Tudors. There in North Wales, in
one of two shires that "cam last into the power of
ẙ *Englishmē*" and "the most roughest, and sharp-
est of al *VVales*, hauynge in it moste highest
Mountaynes," [11]

> Vnder the foot of *Rauran* mossy hore,
> From whence the riuer *Dee* as siluer cleene
> His tombling billowes rolls with gentle rore [12] —

there near the ancient dividing line of "the *Saxon*,
and *Welsh*," [13] a line, according to Lhuyd, still

"accompted at this day one of y͏ͤ auncient bonds, sauing y͏ͭ in certein places, both y͏ͤ people & the welshtongue haue incroched more into England"[14] — there near "a place called *Caergay*, which was the house of *Gay*, *Arthurs* foster brother"[15] — there among the birches Merlin delivered Prince Arthur to be brought up in all the gentle thews and martial might of knighthood. There, in the poet's alembic, Gloriana, England's Tudor Faery Queen "who came from *Arthurs* rase and lyne,"[16] found the Briton prince asleep and wooed him back to the Faeryland which was Elizabethan England. Maurice Kyffin's clarion call was answered:

> *Ye* Bryttish Poets, *Repeat in Royall Song,*
> (*VVith waightie woords, vsde in King* Arthurs *daies*)
> Th' Imperiall Stock, *from whence your* Queene *hath sprong;*
> *Enstall in verse your* Princesse *lasting prayes.*[17]

Perhaps, then, in spite of Rabelais, Lancelot is not yet entirely busied with roasting horses in hell; maybe the knights of the Round Table are still mincing jargonelles and chancing upon kisses from faery mistresses, rather than receiving fillips on the nose and pieces of mouldy bread for ferrying damned souls across the Styx.

NOTES

CHAPTER I

1. Ed. *The Faerie Queene*, Book I, 1915, p. lxviii.

2. The same, p. xlii. Cf. "The Arthurian Empire in the Elizabethan Poets," *Aberystwyth Studies*, IV (1922), 59–66.

3. *Observations on the Fairy Queen of Spenser*, 2nd ed., 1762, I, 28–31.

4. "Spenser's Fairy Mythology," *Studies in Philology*, XV (1918), 106.

5. "A Sixteenth Century Battle of the Books," Program for the 44th Meeting of the Modern Language Association of America, 1927, p. 4.

6. "Materials for the Study of the English Renaissance," *Modern Language Notes*, XLII (1927), 182–183.

7. All references to Spenser's life, unless otherwise stated, follow the consensus as given in Frederic I. Carpenter's *Reference Guide to Edmund Spenser*, 1923, and H. S. V. Jones's *Spenser Handbook*, 1930. All references to Spenser's poems and correspondence will be to the Oxford one-volume edition, 1926, ed. J. C. Smith and E. de Sélincourt (hereafter referred to as Oxford *Spenser*). All references to Spenser's prose tract, *A Veue of the Present State of Ireland*, "finys 1596," will be to Volume IX of *The Complete Works in Verse and Prose of Edmund Spenser*, ed. Grosart, 1882–84 (hereafter referred to as Grosart *Spenser*).

8. *Edmund Spenser*, Paris, 1923, p. 2.

9. A thorough account of the Arthurian legend in the English Renaissance is a desideratum. The following accounts which touch upon the various features may be consulted: M. W. MacCallum, *Tennyson's Idylls of the King and Arthurian Story from the XVIth Century*, 1894; R. P. Wülker, *Die Arthursage in der englischen Literatur*, Leipzig, 1895; Ludwig Oehninger, *Die Verbreitung der Königssagen der Historia Regum Britanniae von Geoffrey of Monmouth in der poetischen*

elisabethanischen Literatur, Munich, 1903; R. H. Fletcher, *The Arthurian Material in the Chronicles* ([*Harvard*] *Studies and Notes in Philology and Literature*, X), 1906; W. L. Jones, "Geoffrey of Monmouth and the Legend of Arthur," *Quarterly Review*, Vol. 205, No. 408 (July, 1906), pp. 54–78; G. H. Maynadier, *The Arthur of the English Poets*, 1907; R. S. Crane, *The Vogue of Medieval Chivalric Romance during the English Renaissance* (abstract of University of Pennsylvania thesis, 1911), 1919; W. E. Mead, "Arthurian Story in the Sixteenth Century," in his ed. of *Chinon of England*, etc. (Early English Text Society, Original Series, No. 165), 1925, pp. xxv–xlvi; Elise F. W. M. van der Ven-Ten Bensel, *The Character of King Arthur in English Literature*, Amsterdam, 1925; K. F. Plesner, *Engelsk Arthur-Digtning* (*Studier fra Sprog-og Oldtidsforskning*, Nr. 136), Copenhagen, 1926; E. K. Chambers, *Arthur of Britain*, 1927. On Spenser's specific debt to the legend, consult the items mentioned in Carpenter's *Reference Guide*, and Alice Parrott's "Critical Bibliography of Spenser from 1923–1928," *Studies in Philology*, XXV (1928), 468–490. To these should be added Miss Winstanley's article in *Aberystwyth Studies*, IV (1922), 60; Professor Greenlaw's "Britomart at the House of Busirane," *Studies in Philology*, XXVI (1929), 124–128; and my "Spenser and the Arthurian Legend," *Review of English Studies*, VI (1930), 167–174.

10. *Edmund Spenser, An Essay on Renaissance Poetry*, 1925, p. 2.

CHAPTER II

1. Ed. Sommer, 1889, I, 1.

2. On the affiliation of the Angevin dynasty to Arthur and on the Anglicization of Arthur, see Chambers, *Arthur of Britain*, pp. 124 ff. Henry II was involved in several unsuccessful Welsh wars, and during the Barons' War Wales became practically independent. A. E. Parsons says that Jusserand (see *The English Novel in the Time of Shakespeare*, ed. 1890, pp. 40 ff.) was the first to suggest "that the adoption of Arthur as national hero was the result of a considered policy on the part

of the Norman rulers to further the amalgamation of races within the island." "The Trojan Legend in England," *Modern Language Review*, XXIV (1929), 257. Arthur, son of Geoffrey of Anjou and Constance of Brittany, was born on March 29, 1187. A register records: "Natus est Arturus filius Gauffridi ducis Britanniae, *desideratus gentibus*." A. Le Moyne de la Borderie, *Histoire de Bretaigne*, 1896–1914, III (1899), 286, note 2; quoted by Chambers, *Arthur of Britain*, p. 112. On young Arthur, who was done away with by John Lackland in 1203, see de la Borderie, III, 286 ff. The Angevin plans for empire were dealt a severe blow when John lost Normandy and much more.

3. David Powel, *The historie of Cambria*, 1584, p. 374.

4. The victorious Edward, according to the *Annals of Waverly*, received the crown of Arthur: "[1283] Item corona famosi regis Arthuri, qui apud Wallenses a longo tempore in maximo honore habebatur, cum aliis iocalibus pretiosis domino regi est oblata; et sic Wallensium gloria ad Anglicos, licet invite, est translata" (text in Chambers, *Arthur of Britain*, p. 279; see also p. 124). But the confidence of the Welsh rebels in Arthur's return, according to the monk of Malmesbury's *Vita Edwardi Secundi*, remained unshaken: "[1315] Porro ex dictis Merlini prophetae sperant adhuc Angliam recuperare. Hinc est quod frequenter insurgunt Walenses, effectum vaticinii implere volentes; sed quia debitum tempus ignorant saepe decipiuntur et in vanum laborant" (text in Chambers, p. 281; see also p. 124). Edward I began his more determined conquest of Wales in 1276. Llewelyn met his death as a result of an insurrection led by him and his brother David in 1282. David was hanged, drawn, and quartered in September, 1283. See George Peele's play, *The Famous Chronicle of king Edward the first*, 1593, commonly known as "Longshankes," in which there occurs a fanciful account of the "life of Lleullen rebell in Wales." In 1284 Wales was formally annexed to England, and after that date the title of "Prince of Wales" was generally given to the heir of the English crown. "Llywelyn ap Grufford," under the date of 1267, heads the list of the Princes of Wales on a tablet in Carnarvon Castle. The suc-

cession of the Princes of Wales to the days of the Tudors is given as follows: Edward of Carnarvon, 1301; Edward the Black Prince, 1344; Richard of Bordeaux, 1370; Henry of Monmouth, 1399; Edward of Westminster, 1454; Edward (afterwards Edward V), 1471; and Edward, son of Richard III, 1483. "*Edward Caernaruon*, first Prince of *Wales* of the English blood," is the first of "The Princes of Wales of the blood *royall of England*" in Powel's *Historie of Cambria*, pp. 376–390, and "Edward of VVindsore" (afterwards Edward III) is included.

5. Powel, *The historie of Cambria*, p. 390. There were two great families of *Tudors*: one of South Wales, *Tewdwr* (L. *Theodorus*); the other of North Wales, *Tudur* (L. *tutor*), which is generally referred to as the Penmynydd, Anglesey, branch, and from which Henry Tudor was directly descended. See W. Garmon Jones, "Welsh Nationalism and Henry Tudor," *Transactions of the Honourable Society of Cymmrodorion* (Session for 1917–18), 1919, p. 30, note 2.

6. Edward Hall, *The Vnion of the two noble and illustrate famelies of Lancastre & Yorke*, ed. Richard Grafton, 1548, sig. Y. iiij.

7. Hall (*ibid.*) thus refers to Owen and Catherine: "This woman, after the death of kyng Henry the fifth her husbande, beyng young and lusty, folowyng more her awne appetite, then frendley counsaill, and regardyng more her priuate affeccion, then her open honour, toke to husband priuily, a goodly gentilman, & a beautyful person, garnished with many Godly gyftes, both of nature & of grace, called Owen Teuther."

8. In 1436 Owen's children were taken from Catherine, and Owen was imprisoned in Newgate. Owen escaped, was retaken, escaped again, and retired to North Wales. A faithful Lancastrian, Owen was at length taken prisoner at the battle of Mortimer's Cross on February 4, 1461, and by order of Edward, Earl of March (afterwards Edward IV), was beheaded in the market-place of Hereford. He was buried at Hereford in a chapel of the church of the Grey Friars. Catherine died in Bermondsey Abbey on January 3, 1437. On the inscription of her altar-tomb erected by Henry VI in the Lady

Chapel of Westminster Abbey, no reference was made to her marriage with Owen Tudor. For some further account of Owen's life, see *DNB.* and J. Williams, "Penmynydd and the Tudors," *Archaeologia Cambrensis,* Third Series, XV (1869), 394–402. For a pedigree of Owen, see British Museum MS. Harl. 1160, ff. 121 ff., and "The .32. auncestors of Owen Tudyr. reduced in to a table of rundelets," in George Owen Harry's *Genealogy of the High and Mighty Monarch, Iames,* 1604. A story connected with Sir Tudor Vaughan ap Grono (or Grono Vaughan ap Tudor), Owen's paternal grandfather, up to whose time the Tudor coat of arms was "a chevron between three Saxons' heads couped" ("three close helmets" in Elizabethan days), illustrates the Tudor prepossession with Arthur: "Sir" Tudor upon being summoned by Edward III for having assumed to himself the honor of knighthood answered that "by the laws and constitution of King Arthur, he had the liberty of taking upon himself that title, in regard that he had those three qualifications which, whoever was endued with, could by those laws claim the honour of a knight. First, he was a gentleman; second, he had sufficient estate; and thirdly, he was valiant and adventurous" (quoted by J. Williams, p. 288, without citation).

9. Edmund Tudor died at Carmarthen, South Wales, on November 3, 1456, and was buried there in the church of the Grey Friars.

10. A. F. Pollard, *The Reign of Henry VII,* 1913–14, II (1914), 6–8. According to Froissart, the House of Lancaster received the crown from the Plantagenets in fulfilment of a prophecy of Merlin. See A. E. Parsons, "The Trojan Legend in England," *Modern Language Review,* XXIV (1929), 263. Through his paternal grandmother, the wife of "Sir" Tudor Vaughan ap Grono, Owen Tudor traced his descent from Edward I.

11. In an oration to his soldiers on the field of battle Richard considered that the very devil had "entered into the harte of an vnknowen welshman" with his "beggerly Britons" (Hall, *The Vnion of Lancastre & Yorke,* sig. [II .viᵛ]). A gloss of E. K.'s in the May eclogue of *The Shepheardes Calender,* re-

ferring to Lord Hastings, in Richard III's days, being "of the Tyranne put to a shamefull deathe," may be considered indirect commendation of Henry (Oxford *Spenser*, p. 440).

12. William Martyn, *The Historie and Liues, of the Kings of England*, 1628, p. 323.

13. W. Garmon Jones, "Welsh Nationalism and Henry Tudor," *Transactions of the Honourable Society of Cymmrodorion* (Session for 1917–18), 1919, pp. 17–18. See pp. 41–59 for original texts referring to Henry as "Tarw Du" and "Tarw Mon" (or "Tarw o Fon").

14. Hall, *The Vnion of Lancastre & Yorke*, sig. aaa. i^v; quoted without citation by Frederick J. Harries, *The Welsh Elizabethans*, Pontypridd, 1924, p. 31.

15. Lewis Einstein, *Tudor Ideals*, 1921, p. 3.

16. Known also as Lewis Y Glyn, or Llewelyn Glyn Cothi, a native of Glyn Cothi in Carmarthenshire who flourished during the reigns of Henry VI, Edward IV, Richard III, and Henry VII. Charles Wilkins says: "Glyn Cothi is inseparably associated with the long course of events, the blending of Welsh warriors with Yorkists and Lancastrians in the civil wars of England, and that more durable annexation of Wales with England which resulted from the placing of a Tudor on the throne" (*The History of the Literature of Wales from the Year 1300 to the Year 1650*, 1884, pp. 112–113).

17. Ode XI in "Y Dosparth VIII," *Gwaith Lewis Glyn Cothi* (*The Poetical Works of Lewis Glyn Cothi*), ed. [John Jones and Walter Davies] for The Cymmrodorion, or Royal Cambrian Institution, 1837, lines 1–20, 45–60, 77–88, pp. 497–500. The reference (line 10) to "Siaspar Dug o Bedfort" sets October 27, 1485, as the *terminus a quo* for the completion of the poem, for Jasper Tudor was created Duke of Bedford on that date.

18. Caroline A. J. Skeel, "Wales under Henry VII," *Tudor Studies Presented to Albert Frederick Pollard*, ed. R. W. Seton-Watson, 1924, p. 22.

19. Henry Chettle (?), *Englandes Mourning Garment: Worne here by plaine Shepheardes; in memorie of their sacred Mistresse Elizabeth*, no date, sig. [A4^v]. For further testimony

of the spirit in which Henry was received, see Bernard André, "Vita Henrici VII," ed. James Gairdner in *Memorials of King Henry the Seventh*, Rolls Series, 1858, p. 9; Charles Dunster, notes on John Philips' *Cider*, 1791, p. 165; W. Llewelyn Williams, "The Union of England and Wales," *Transactions of the Honourable Society of Cymmrodorion* (Session for 1907–08), 1909, pp. 68–74; W. Garmon Jones, "Welsh Nationalism and Henry Tudor," the same (Session for 1917–18), 1919, pp. 24 ff., 40–41.

20. Gwenllian, the great-granddaughter of Rhys, was the second wife of Ednyfed Vychan, from which union Owen Tudor was directly descended. Henry's descent from Rhys was mentioned in verse (Jones, the same, p. 30, note 3). Despite the fact that Henry was born in Pembroke Castle, South Wales, he was considered a Northwallian.

21. Southwallians during the disturbances of the reign of Henry VI were principally attached to the House of York, whereas the Northwallians were attached to the House of Lancaster. The contending parties united under Henry Tudor. Henry VII and Henry VIII are thus praised in the April eclogue of *The Shepheardes Calender* in the gloss on "The Redde rose medled with the White yfere": "By the mingling of the Redde rose and the White, is meant the vniting of the two principall houses of Lancaster and of Yorke: by whose longe discord and deadly debate, this realm many yeares was sore traueiled, and almost cleane decayed. Til the famous Henry the seuenth, of the line of Lancaster, taking to wife the most vertuous Princesse Elisabeth, daughter to the fourth Edward of the house of Yorke, begat the most royal Henry the eyght . . ., in whom was the firste vnion of the Whyte Rose and the Redde" (Oxford *Spenser*, p. 434).

22. John Leland, *Collectanea*, ed. Hearne, 1770, IV, 218.

23. "KAtherina Valesia filia Caroli sexti Regis Francorum, vxor Henrici quinti, quo mortuo, cepit in maritum Oenum Theodorum nobilē Cambrobritannum qui genus suum ad Cadwalladrum referebat" (*Reges, Reginae, Nobiles, et alij in Ecclesia Collegiata B. Petri Westmonasterij sepulti*, ed. [William Camden], 1603, sig. C). The omniscient Pepys and his wife

saw Catherine's remains when they visited the royal tombs on February 23, 1669: "Here we did see, by particular favour, the body of Queen Katherine of Valois; and I had the upper part of her body in my hands, and I did kiss her mouth, reflecting upon it that I did kiss a Queen, and that this was my birthday, thirty-six years old, that I did first kiss a Queen. But here this man, who seems to understand well, tells me that the saying is not true that says she was never buried, for she was buried; only, when Henry the Seventh built his chapel, it was taken up and laid in this wooden coffin [near the tomb of Henry V]; but I did there see that, in it, the body was buried in a leaden one, which remains under the body to this day" (*Diary*, ed. Wheatley, 1896–99, VIII, 222–223). Braybrooke states (the same, p. 222, note 2) that the body was "at length removed from the public gaze into St. Nicholas's chapel, and finally deposited under the monument of Sir George Villiers, when the vault was made for the remains of Elizabeth Percy, Duchess of Northumberland, in December, 1776." The body was apparently reburied in the chantry of Henry V in 1878.

24. The real cause was perhaps Richard III's formal proclamation against Henry on June 23, 1485, that Henry had no legitimate claim to the throne: "for he is discended of bastard blood bothe of ffather side and of mother side" (Pollard, *The Reign of Henry VII*, I, 4). Cf. Richard's letter of June 21, 1485, in Lewis Dwnn's *Tair Sir Deheubarth*, etc., 1586–1613, ed. Sir Samuel R. Meyrick, *Heraldic Visitations of Wales*, for the Welsh Manuscripts Society, Llandovery, 1846, I, xx.

25. Powel, *The historie of Cambria*, p. 391. Powel objects to "the reprochfull and slanderous assertions" of those who would "abase the noble parentage of the said *Owen* this kings grandfather." Gairdner writes: "It is evident that either from policy or natural inclination Henry loved to hear his ancient pedigree talked about" (*Memorials of King Henry the Seventh*, Rolls Series, 1858, p. lx).

26. William Wynne, *The History of Wales* (a new edition, with appendix, of Powel's *Historie*), 1697, p. 334. British Museum MS. Add. 27,965 (early 16th century), a vellum sheet with arms roughly drawn in color, showing the descent of Eng-

lish kings from Richard II to Henry VII, gives in one circle
"Owen ap Meredeth-Tuder proud husband to-Catharin
queene of Englond."

27. George Gordon, "The Trojans in Britain," *Essays and
Studies by Members of the English Association*, IX (1924), 28.
According to the mediæval legend, Brutus was the great-
grandson of Æneas. The line ran as follows: Æneas, Ascanius,
Silvius, and Brutus. Gordon states (the same, p. 29) that in
all the branches of the Trojan story the "Welsh House of
Tudor had almost a duty . . ., for its arms were supported by
the British Dragon."

28. A. E. Parsons, "The Trojan Legend in England," *Modern Language Review*, XXIV (1929), 253–254.

29. Of Cadwalader, who died apparently in the great plague
of 664, Chambers states (*Arthur of Britain*, p. 218): "There
does not appear to be any evidence that he was in fact looked
to in popular belief as a deliverer. His coming is still the subject of prophecy in the *Vita Merlini*." But for evidence to the
contrary, see Skene, *The Four Ancient Books of Wales*, 1868, I,
75, and J. E. Lloyd, *A History of Wales from the Earliest Times
to the Edwardian Conquest*, 1911, I, 230. Pertinent lines in the
"Hoianau," *The Black Book of Caermarthen*, XVIII (Skene, II,
26), are quoted by Lloyd (I, 230, note 8):

> A phan del Kadualadir y orescin mon
> dileaur Saeson o tirion prydein.

("And when Cadwaladr comes to seize Anglesey, the English
will be driven from the pleasant isle of Britain.") One of
"Marueilous Merling's" prophecies has the following lines:

> One thousand and more after Christes birth,
> When the Calnalider [*sic*] of Cornwell is called
> And the Wolfe out of Wailes is vanquisht for aye:
> Then many ferlies shall fall, and many folke die.

*The Whole Prophecies of Scotland, England, France, Ireland
and Denmarke*, ed. 1617, sig. A2. See also William Harbert
(or William Herbert) of Glamorgan's poem, *A Prophesie of
Cadwallader, last king of the Britaines*, 1604. The frequent
reference to Cadwalader is due in part to his having been the

last king of the Britons. It should also be noted that a revival of Welsh prophetic literature coincided with the activities of Rhys ap Tudor and Griffith ap Conan in the eleventh century. These heroes were then expected to return to life and expel the English. By the twelfth century it was definitely Arthur who was to restore the British empire.

30. Sir John Doddridge, "A Consideration of the Office and Duty of the Heralds in England, drawn out of sundry Observations," a paper presented before the Elizabethan Society of Antiquaries in August, 1600, ed. Hearne, *Curious Discourses*, 1773, I, 164.

31. Angharad Llwyd, *A History of the Island of Mona*, Ruthin, 1833, p. 330, note*.

32. *The Historie of the Reigne of King Henry the Seventh*, ed. 1641, pp. 18–19. Cf. H. A. L. Fisher, *The History of England from the Accession of Henry VII. to the Death of Henry VIII.* (*The Political History of England*, ed. Hunt and Poole, V), 1906, p. 13.

33. *Ioannis Twini Bolingdunensis, Angli, de Rebus Albionicis, Britannicis atque Anglicis, Commentariorum libri duo*, ed. Thomas Twyne, 1590, sigg. M–M^v.

34. J. C. Walters says that the association of Arthur with Winchester led Henry to name his son "after the Arthur of romance" (*The Lost Land of King Arthur*, 1909, p. 140). T. W. Shore says, furthermore, that Henry saw to it that his first child should be born at Winchester ("King Arthur and the Round Table at Winchester," reprinted from the *Hampshire Field Club Papers and Proceedings*, 1900, p. 196). George Borrow states: "The ardent Welsh, on hearing that the presumptive heir to the throne was named after the British hero of old, were delighted and said: 'Merlin was a prophet after all and Arthur shall yet come to reign over fair Britain'" (*Celtic Bards, Chiefs and Kings*, ed. H. G. Wright, 1928, p. 140). The Round Table at Winchester (*ca.* seventeen feet in diameter) hangs to the present time at the west end of the Great Hall, above the remains of the royal dais. See Melville Portal, *The Great Hall, Winchester Castle*, 1899. Muirhead states that the

old Table is "said to have existed in the 13th cent. and possibly older," and he adds that "it was repainted in the reign of Henry VII" (perhaps in honor of the birth of Prince Arthur?). According to Chambers (*Arthur of Britain*, pp. 131–132), the Table, probably "a relic of some joust or pageant," is first mentioned in John Hardyng's *Chronicle* (15th century).

35. Skelton's poem, no copy of which is known to exist, is mentioned in the laureate's *Garlande or Chapelet of Laurell*, line 1178, in the answer of "Occupacyoun" to the "Quene of Fame" (*The Poetical Works of John Skelton*, ed. Dyce, 1843, I, 408). A section entitled "Arthur" is devoted to Arthur, Prince of Wales, in Powel's discussion of "the Princes of Wales of the blood *royall of England*" in *The historie of Cambria*, pp. 390–392. In the list of the Princes of Wales on a tablet in Carnarvon Castle he appears as "Arthur Tudor, 1489." For the precise date of his creation as Prince of Wales, see William Campbell, *Materials for a History of Henry VII.*, Rolls Series, 1873–77, II (1877), 541 ff.

36. "Vita Henrici VII," ed. Gairdner in *Memorials of Henry the Seventh*, p. 41.

37. The same, p. 44.

38. *Genethliacon in illustrissimū principē. D. arturū*, British Museum MS. Harl. 336, ff. 83ᵛ–84.

39. *Aliud epigrāma de noīē arturi indito ipī Sereᵐᵒ principi*, British Museum MS. Harl. 336, f. 83.

40. *Suasoria Lęticię ad angliam pro sublatis bellis ciuilibus et Arthuro prīcipe nato epistola*, British Museum MS. Add. 33,376 (formerly Grenville x), ff. 10ᵛ–11. The manuscript, beautifully illuminated, shows at the bottom of f. 2 the Red Dragon of Cadwalader breathing fire.

41. Robert Withington, *English Pageantry*, 1918–20, I (1918), 164.

42. *The Historie of the Reigne of King Henry the Seventh*, ed. 1641, p. 205.

43. "Vita Henrici VII," ed. Gairdner in *Memorials of Henry the Seventh*, p. 10.

44. I. H., *A Treatise of Vnion of the two Realmes of England and Scotland*, 1604, p. 55.

45. William Drummond, *The History of Scotland*, 1655, p. 133.

46. *Stemma Regum Scotiae*, British Museum MS. Harl. 289, f. 190. Of the several Arthurs who were dukes of Brittany, special attention should be called again to Arthur Plantagenet, the grandson of Henry II. Frequent mention of this unfortunate prince is made throughout the Renaissance. See Claude Paradin, *Alliances Genialogiques des Rois et Princes de Gaule*, Lyons, 1561, pp. 252 ff., and Powel, *The historie of Cambria*, p. 253. Hall makes several references to a Renaissance "Arthur Plantagenet" (*The Vnion of Lancastre & Yorke*, ff. xxxij ff.).

47. Richard Robinson, *A Learned and True Assertion of Prince Arthure*, 1582, sig. A4ᵛ.

48. *A petegre of Henry the eyght from the princes of Wales by father and mother made . . . in the .7 yeare of Henry the eyght*, British Museum MS. Cotton Julius F. ix, ff. 24–24ᵛ.

49. George Borrow, *Celtic Bards, Chiefs and Kings*, ed. Wright, 1928, p. 192. Though Borrow does exaggerate, nevertheless the assumption of the name is specifically mentioned as one count in the indictment preferred against the Welsh prince: "novum nomen videlicet Ryce ap Gruffith ffitzuryen in se proditorie assumpsit." See W. Llewelyn Williams, "A Welsh Insurrection," *Y Cymmrodor*, XVI (1903), 38, 43.

50. Shore, "King Arthur and the Round Table at Winchester," p. 199; Chambers, *Arthur of Britain*, p. 132.

51. Hall, *The Vnion of Lancastre & Yorke*, sig. [OOo.v].

52. *Lordonnance et ordre du tournoy/ ioustes/ de combat/ a pied/ & a cheual. . . . Les ditz & deuiz . . . a calaix*, [1520], sig. fᵛ.

53. *Le triūphe festifz bien venue & honorable recoeul faict per le Roy dāgleterre en la ville de Calais*, Arras, 1520, sigg. [B]–[Bᵛ].

54. Shore, "King Arthur and the Round Table at Winchester," p. 198. Lord Herbert of Cherbury quotes the motto as "Cui adhaereo praeest" (*The Life and Raigne of King Henry the Eighth*, 1649, p. 98).

55. Withington, *English Pageantry*, I, 177; quoted from Corpus Christi (Cambridge) MS. 298.(8).

56. *The Vnion of Lancastre & Yorke*, 1548, sig. RRr.iᵛ.

57. Shore, "King Arthur and the Round Table at Winchester," p. 198.

58. Ed. W. E. Mead, together with Richard Robinson's English translation, 1582, and Christopher Middleton's *Chinon of England* (Early English Text Society, Original Series, No. 165), 1925, pp. 91–151. See also Leland's "Codrus, sive Laus & Defensio Gallofridi Arturii Monumetensis contra Polydorum Vergilium," in *Collectanea*, ed. Hearne, 1770, V, 2–10.

59. An English translation was made shortly after the first edition, but was never printed. Many subsequent editions of the Latin appeared. Another book, bringing the history down to 1538, was added to the 1555 edition, which was again printed at Basel. Polydore Vergil (or Polydore de Castello) came to England as a sub-collector of Peter's pence, and undertook his history at the request of Henry VII. He was naturalized in 1510, and died *ca.* 1555. On Polydore, see *Three Books of Polydore Vergil's English History*, ed. Sir Henry Ellis (Camden Society, XXIX), 1844, pp. [i]–xxxii; John Ferguson, "Bibliographical Notes on the English Translation of Polydore Vergil's work 'De Inventoribus Rerum,'" *Archaeologia*, LI (Second Series, I, 1888), 107–141; W. G. Waters, "Pioneers in Humanism," *Anglo-Italian Review*, Vol. III, No. 11 (London, 1919), pp. 250–253; Cardinal F. A. Gasquet, *Monastic Life in the Middle Ages*, 1922, pp. 178–196, a reprint of "Some Materials for a New Edition of Polydore Vergil's 'History,'" *Transactions of the Royal Historical Society*, New Series, XVI (1902), 1–17; E. A. Whitney and P. P. Cram, "The Will of Polydore Vergil," the same, Fourth Series, XI (1928), 117–136.

60. Editions of Geoffrey's *Historia Regum Britanniae* were published by J. Badius Ascensius at Paris in 1508 and 1517. The 1517 edition bears the following title: *Britannię utriusq̃ Regū Et Principum Origo & gesta insignia ab Galfrido Monemutensi ex antiquissimis Britannici sermonis monumentis in latinum traducta: & ab Ascensio rursus maiore accuratione impressa.* See *The Historia Regum Britanniae of Geoffrey of Monmouth*, ed. Acton Griscom, 1929, pp. 10 ff.

61. The happy phrasing is Professor Greenlaw's. See p. 147, note 5, above. The suggestion for the use of the words could well have come from Edmund Bolton's *Hypercritica, ca.* 1618 (in *Critical Essays of the Seventeenth Century*, ed. Spingarn, 1908, I, 87), where the controversy is briefly summarized.

62. Text: translatehe.

63. *Polydore Vergil's English History*, ed. Ellis (Camden Society, XXXVI), 1846, I, 29. The edition has never been completed.

64. The same, pp. 121–122.

65. According to Polydore himself he followed the main features of the old British story "not altogether without indignation." But his realization that he was among Britons served as some check on his critical attitude: "The common people (who allwais more regarde novelties then trewthe) . . . seme to bee in heaven, whear with a good will I will leave them" (the same, p. 33).

66. F. 32ᵛ. Gildas first appeared in print at London (?) in 1525: *Opus Nouum. Gildas Britannus Monachus Cui Sapientis cognomētū est inditum, de calamitate excidio, & conquestu Britanniae, quam Angliam nunc uocant, author uetustus a multis diu desyderatus, & nuper in gratiam. D. Cutheberti Tonstalli, Londineñ. Episcopi formulis excusus. [una cum castigatione in reges, principes et sacerdotes; edente Polydoro Vergilio]*. Thus there was probably an additional complaint against Polydore. Many subsequent editions of Gildas came out. In 1567 ff. appeared editions by John Joscelyn (or Josselin), sometime Latin secretary of Archbishop Matthew Parker.

67. F. 36ᵛ.

68. Preface to Malory's *Morte d'Arthur*, 1485, ed. Sommer, I, 2.

69. F. 37.

70. F. 37ᵛ: "Henricus, felix Octaui nomine uictor," "uindex Arturius alter."

71. *Ibid.*: "ARTVRIVS REDIVIVVS."

72. The first full running title from the supposedly unique copy in the Henry E. Huntington Library at San Marino, California. The copy (an octavo in black letter with register

a-h in eights) bears no title-page, and all pages are missing before sig. a.iii.   The running title varies among "A cōmendacion Of welshmen," "A commendacion Of welshmen," "A
treatise. Of welshmen," and "A treatise. A treatise." No
bibliographer appears to have made a transcript of the title-
page before it was lost.   In his remarks on Kelton, Anthony
à Wood had not seen "another book of poetry in praise of the
Welsh men, dedicated to sir Will. Herbert," or "other (if any)
of his things in prose." *Athenae Oxonienses*, ed. with additions
by Bliss, 1813–20, I (1813), 166.   Bliss (I, 167) attributes the
book to Kelton, echoes Wood with the title *Book of Poetry in
praise of the Welsh men*, and says that it is "one of the scar-
cest in the English language."   Bliss adds: "The copy before
me wants the title-page, but I shall have no hesitation in
attributing it to the press of Grafton, and the last page sup-
plies the date, 1546. It commences on sign. a.iii."   The similarity of the type and the identity of the colophon, except for
the date, with that of Kelton's *Chronycle with a Genealogie
declaryng that the Brittons . . . are lineallye dyscended from
Brute*, 1547, evidently influenced Bliss in naming the printer,
and he is followed doubtfully by Pollard and Redgrave (*Short-
Title Catalogue*, 1926, No. 14919, p. 335).   Professor Godfrey
Davies makes a brief statement: "An examination of the book
itself yielded nothing except that it had once belonged to
B. Bandinel. This strengthens the probability that the Huntington Library copy is the one P. Bliss describes."

The work is composed of 409 doggerel stanzas, exclusive of
ten stanzas of apology, which rime *aabccb*, whenever they can,
and whose lines vary from dimeter to trimeter to tetrameter.
A positive photostatic reproduction of the original is to be
found in my typewritten Ph.D. thesis, *Studies in Spenser and
the Arthurian Legend*, 1930 (II, 381–443), which is deposited in
the Harvard College Library, Cambridge, Massachusetts.
Dr. Max Farrand, Director of Research at the Huntington
Library, has kindly granted permission for the use and reproduction of the desired portion of the work.

73. Sig. a.iiii^v.

74. Sig. c.i^v.

75. Sigg. d.ii–d.ii^v.

76. Sig. d.ii^v.

77. Sig. e.i.

78. Sig. e.iiii.

79. Sig. e.v.

80. Sigg. [e.vi]–[e.vi^v].

81. Sig. [f.iii].

82. Sigg. [f.iii^v]–f.iiii.

83. Outer margin (partly clipped), sig. f.iiii.

84. Sig. [f].v.

85. Outer margin (partly clipped), *ib'd*.

86. Sig. [g.viii^v].

87. Sig. c.iiii^v.

88. Sig. [c.vi^v].

89. Sig. e.ii^v.

90. Sig. b.i^v.

91. F. 84^v. See also f. 85 and the section devoted to "POly-dorus Vergilius," ff. 223–223^v.

92. Sig. Bij^v.

93. Sig. C. v. See the *Genealogię deorum gentilium*, Venice, 1472, Book VI, Section C. lvii: Boccaccio relates the story of Brutus, "quę quoniā mihi nec uera: nec uerisimilia uisa sunt: omittēda cēsui."

94. Sigg. D.i–D.i^v.

95. British Museum MS. Harl. 1074 (16th century), f. 229^v.

96. John Foxe, *The Second Volume of the Ecclesiasticall History, conteyning the Actes & Monumentes of Martyrs*, 1576, p. 1402. Cf. Withington, *English Pageantry*, I, 191, note 2.

97. The same, p. 1406.

98. *Historia de los Reyes Godos que vinieron de la Scythia de Europa contra el Imperio Romano; y a España: con Succession Dellos, hasta los Catolicos Reyes Don Fernando y Doña Isabel* [with additions by "Maestro Fray Geronimo de Castro y Castillo, hijo del Autor"], Madrid, 1624, p. 365; cited by Juan Antonio Pellicer y Pellares, notes to *Don Quixote* (Part I, Chapter 13), ed. Madrid, 1797–98, I (1797), 130.

99. *History of Spanish Literature*, 6th American ed., 1888, I, 263–264. Cf. Maynadier, *The Arthur of the English Poets*, p. 287.

100. Powel, *The historie of Cambria*, p. 393. Apparently *ca.* 1525 Henry VIII styled Mary "Princess of Wales" and sent her to keep court at Ludlow Castle. See *Privy Purse Expenses of the Princess Mary*, ed. Frederick Madden, 1831, p. xxxviii and note. Edward VI, before he became king, was popularly acclaimed "Prince of Wales," but the title was never officially bestowed upon him. Cf. the very title of Leland's poem of 1543: *Genethliacon illustrissimi Eäduerdi Principis Cambriae*.

CHAPTER III

1. Part of the refrain in Thomas Watson's "Nimphes meeting their May Queene," sung by "six virgins" before Elizabeth at Elvetham in 1591 (*Englands Helicon*, 1600, ed. [Hugh Macdonald], 1925, pp. 48–49).

2. The complete reading has kindly been furnished by John Ballinger, Esq., of the National Library of Wales, Aberystwyth. See the *Calendar of Wynn (of Gwydir) Papers, 1515–1690*, ed. [Ballinger], 1926, p. 342. There seems to be in existence no copy of the writ itself, but it is very probable that this Owen Tudor was a close cousin of Henry VII. We do know that there was an Owen Tudor Vychan who was third cousin and "Esg^r of Body to H. 7" (Dwnn, *Tair Sir Deheubarth*, etc., 1586–1613, ed. Meyrick, 1846, II, 191). It is quite possible that this Owen Tudor served both Henry and Arthur, Prince of Wales, in this capacity, for "a number of escheated and forfeited lands in Anglesey were granted out by Arthur Prince of Wales to 'Owen Tudor', his kinsman in blood." J. Williams, "Penmynydd and the Tudors," *Archaeologia Cambrensis*, Third Series, XV (1869), 388. The date given to this grant, 1514, is obviously incorrect, for Arthur Tudor died in 1502.

3. British Museum MS. Stowe 572 (*ca.* 1590), f. 54.

4. Powel, *The historie of Cambria*, p. 318. In the beautifully emblazoned British Museum MS. King's 396 (*ca.* 1570), f. 26, which contains Elizabeth's descent from Robert, Duke

of Normandy, Owen Tudor appears as "The Noble Owen of Wales descended lineally as heire male of Cadwalider kinge of Britayne." In British Museum MS. Harl. 2129 (16th century), f. 30ᵛ (renumbered 45ᵛ), is shown Elizabeth's descent from "the noble owen tuther." Genealogies of Elizabeth in manuscript abound in Welsh as well as in English. One example from the Welsh will suffice: "ELISABETH verch Harri wythfed ab Harri saithfed, ab Edmont iarll Richmond ab Owen ab Mredith ab Tydyr . . . ab Britis ab Silis ab Esganys ab Eneas ysgwyddwyn" (Dwnn, *Tair Sir Deheubarth*, etc., 1586–1613, ed. Meyrick, II, 11).

5. Notes to Drayton's *Poly-Olbion*, 1612, Song 2, p. 35.

6. Sir Egerton Brydges, *The British Bibliographer*, 1810–14, I (1810), 339. The broadside was licensed to Richard Jones as "a ballat of brittishe Sidanen applied by a courtier to ye praise of ye Quene." See H. E. Rollins, *An Analytical Index to the Ballad-Entries (1557–1709) in the Registers of the Company of Stationers of London*, 1924, No. 249, pp. 29–30. Professor Rollins points out that Sidanen is a character in Anthony Mundy's play *John a Kent and John a Cumber*, and he gives other references to her. He contributes the additional information that she is said to have been the daughter-in-law of Llewelyn ap Iorwerth, whose son Griffith she married. See *Notes and Queries*, IV (1851), 120, 424. If the report be true, Sidanen, a heroine famed for her great beauty, was the sister-in-law of the still more famous Gladys Ddu and the mother of Llewelyn ap Griffith, the last native Prince of Wales. The Welsh word *sidanen* is properly an adjective meaning "silken" (from *sidan*, "silk"), and it came to be a complimentary epithet for a lady. In Lloyd's broadside the compliment is turned to Elizabeth: she is Sidanen by virtue of her Tudor descent.

7. Printed marginal note on "Puissant Princesse," sig. Bᵛ.

8. Sig. *2ᵛ.

9. Sigg. D3ᵛ, D3.

10. "Of the Antiquity of Arms in England," *Curious Discourses*, ed. Hearne, 1773, I, 114. The crest of Wales at the present time is a dragon passant guardant, gules.

11. *Flores Historiarum*, Frankfort, 1601, pp. 94–95.

12. Holinshed's *Chronicles*, ed. 1808, IV, 645. See John Upton, ed. *The Faerie Queene*, 1758, II, 332.

13. *Original Letters*, ed. Ellis, Second Series, 1827, III, 135–136.

14. On the vogue of the Nine Worthies, which was set by Jacques de Longuyon's *Vœux du Paon* (*ca.* 1310), see Sir Israel Gollancz, preface and appendix to his ed. of *The Parlement of the Thre Ages*, 1915 (first printed for the Roxburghe Club in 1897), and John Barbour's *Buik of Alexander*, ed. R. L. Græme Ritchie, Scottish Text Society, 1921–29, I (1925), pp. xl ff. and notes. The popularity of the vogue and the extension of the original idea in the English Renaissance is shown, not only by countless allusions, but also by the following separate works: Richard Lloyd, *A briefe discourse of the Nine worthies*, 1584; Richard Johnson, *The nine Worthies of London*, 1592; and Robert Fletcher, *The Nine English Worthies*, 1606. Arthur, "Fyrst and chyef of the thre best crysten," strides worthily everywhere, and England gained another among the Nine by including Guy of Warwick. At one time or another each of the Tudor kings figured as a Tenth Worthy.

15. Ritchie (ed. Barbour's *Buik of Alexander*, I, p. xli, note 8) refers to a forthcoming work on the Nine Women Worthies by Miss Aileen A. Calderwood. From Lydgate to Thomas Middleton the Nine Muses appear with the Nine Worthies, and since Lydgate did not originate anything, the idea for the Nine Women Worthies is obviously older. See Withington, *English Pageantry*, I, 138, and note 4. We regret with Professor Kittredge that the "worthy" Wife of Bath did not take time to give us a list, including herself. In *The Exemplary Lives and Memorable Acts of Nine the Most Worthy Women of the World*, 1640, Thomas Heywood says that the idea for nine alludes "to the number of the Muses," and "*Elizabeth*, Queene of *England, France and Ireland, &c.* Defender of the Faith," is included as "the last of the rest in time and place, though equall to any of the former both in religious vertue, and all masculine magnanimity." See Heywood's *Life of Merlin, Sirnamed Ambrosius*, 1641, p. 346.

16. Humphrey Lhuyd, *The Breuiary of Britayne*, ed. Thomas Twyne, 1573, f. 89ᵛ. Spenser was fond of Boadicea. He not only deviates from Geoffrey of Monmouth's *Historia* to include her in the chronicle account of Book II of *The Faerie Queene*, but also at the end of the chronicle account in Book III he returns to the same theme. He also devotes a stanza to her in *The Ruines of Time*, placing her there alongside of "stout *Pendragon*." Professor Renwick (ed. *Complaints*, 1928, p. 193) says that in having Boadicea assail Verulam, Spenser "deliberately falsifies history . . . and seems careless of aught but the effect to be produced." Thomas Heywood includes Boadicea in his account of the Nine Women Worthies in 1640, and in *The Life of Merlin*, 1641, p. 329, he states of the accession of Mary I: "Now ceased the Heire Male to Reign, and the Scepter was disposed to the Female, which was not seen nor known, since long before the Conquest: when *Bouduca* [*sic*], or as some call her *Boadicia* soveraignized."

17. John Ferne, *The Blazon of Gentrie*, 1586, Part I, p. 157.

18. Part II, p. 129. References of this nature could be multiplied. In *Aue Caesar. God saue the King*, 1603, sig. Aiiij, Elizabeth is a Judith and a Deborah. In Thomas Gainsford's *Vision and Discourse of Henry the seuenth*, 1610, p. 3, she is England's Deborah.

19. Dedicatory epistle, reprint of 1814 (no signatures, no pagination). The title-page is faced by a portrait of Elizabeth. Cf. Carpenter's *Reference Guide*, p. 244.

20. *The Life of Merlin*, 1641, p. 346.

21. *Autobiographical Tracts of Dr. John Dee*, ed. James Crossley, Chetham Miscellanies, I (Chetham Society Publications, XXIV), 1851, p. 74. See also p. 25.

22. *The Private Diary of Dr. John Dee*, ed. Halliwell (Camden Society, XIX), 1842, p. 9.

23. *Ibid.* See also *The Compendious Rehearsall of John Dee*, Chetham Miscellanies, I, 1851, pp. 18–19.

24. British Museum MS. Lansd. 94, art. 51, ff. 121–122ᵛ.

25. The same, f. 121.

26. *Ibid.*

27. Ff. 137ᵛ–138. Some idea of Dee's report may be gained from the badly damaged British Museum MS. Cotton Otho C. vii, art. 3.

28. The extensive commentary of Alanus de Insulis was prepared *ca.* 1167–83, and was first published at Frankfort in 1603. A second edition came out in 1608.

29. Text: iu.

30. F. 135ᵛ.

31. *Diary*, ed. Halliwell, p. 4.

32. P. 35.

33. P. 56.

34. P. 55. It is significant that Dee makes for Edgar the apology of "being, but a Saxon."

35. P. 8.

36. Pp. 24–25.

37. *Diary*, ed. Halliwell, p. 4.

38. *Ibid.* Cf. E. G. R. Taylor, *Tudor Geography*, 1930, p. 123.

39. Oxford *Spenser*, p. 632.

40. See *DNB*. Rogers, a naturalized Englishman, was on various missions in the diplomatic service of Elizabeth from 1566 to 1588. He died in 1591. In a letter to Sidney from Frankfort, December 26, 1577, Languet refers to Rogers as "the envoy of your most gracious Queen" and as one of "my dearest friends, and your greatest admirers" (*The Correspondence of Philip Sidney and Hubert Languet*, ed. W. A. Bradley, 1912, p. 146; see also pp. 144, 149, 167). Cf. Sidney to Languet, March 1, 1578 (the same, p. 159).

41. *The Works of Gabriel Harvey*, ed. Grosart, 1884, I, 127.

42. "1577. Jan. 16th, the Erle of Lecester, Mr. Phillip Sydney, Mr. Dyer, &c., came to my howse" (*Diary*, ed. Halliwell, p. 2; see also pp. 5, 20). Sidney was knighted in 1583; Dyer, in 1596.

43. College of Arms (London) MS. Arundel I, f. 73ᵛ.

44. "[1579] July 13th, Arthurus Dee natus puer mane hor. 4 min. 30 fere, vel potius min. 25, in ipso ortu solis, ut existimo" (*Diary*, ed. Halliwell, p. 6).

45. Pp. 243–244. Hakluyt gives the Latin with an English translation from "*Lib.* 9, *cap.* 10.," "*Lib.* 9, *cap.* 12.," and

"*Lib.* 9, *cap.* 19.," and the edition of Geoffrey used is that by Hieronimus Commelinus: "Galfredi Monumetensis, cognomento: Arturi de origine & gestis Regum Britanniae Libri XII," in *Rerum Britannicarum, Id Est Angliae, Scotiae, Vicinarumque Insularum Ac Regionum, Scriptores Vetustiores Ac Praecipui,* Heidelberg, 1587, pp. 1–92.

46. *The Second Part of the principall Nauigations,* 1589, p. 245. On p. 244 Hakluyt gives Lambard's Latin.

47. Text: partibis.

48. *Prophetia Anglicana,* Frankfort, 1603, pp. 22–23.

49. *Historie of Ireland, ca.* 1571, ed. Sir James Ware, together with Meredith Hanmer's *Chronicle of Ireland,* Henry Marleburrough's *Chronicle of Ireland,* and Spenser's *View of Ireland,* 1633 (two issues with a different leading title-page), p. 28 (sig. C2).

50. Grosart *Spenser,* IX, 78.

51. Lilian Winstanley, ed. *The Faerie Queene,* Book I, p. xlii. Cf. *Aberystwyth Studies,* IV (1922), 61.

52. *The chronicle of Ihon Hardyng,* ed. Richard Grafton, 1543, sig. [h.viii^v].

53. Text: Emperonre.

54. *The chronicle of Ihon Hardyng,* 1543, sig. k.

55. See Fletcher, *The Arthurian Material in the Chronicles,* 1906, pp. 251 ff., 264 ff.

56. From "The Author to his booke," sig. D2. Examples of this nature could be multiplied. See also Greenlaw, "Spenser and British Imperialism," *Modern Philology,* IX (1911–12), 347–370.

57. Henry Morley, *English Writers,* VIII, 360.

58. "Virgil and Spenser," *University of California Publications in English,* II (1929), 329. See "Le Bocage Royal," in *Oeuvres Complètes de P. de Ronsard,* ed. Prosper Blanchemain, 1857–67, III (1858), 323–337.

59. Sig. [B4].

60. Pp. 103–104; ed. 1587, pp. 123–124; ed. 1590, pp. 159–160. Professor J. W. Draper would like to think this the passage which caused Spenser to pitch "upon Arthur as the super-hero of his poem." See "The Narrative Technique of

the *Faerie Queene," Publications of the Modern Language Association of America*, XXXIX (1924), 323. Bishop Hall hails Spenser, Sidney, and Camden as "three of a kind, all bred by that England which Camden makes known, to the envy of Spain." See Helen E. Sandison, "Three Spenser Allusions," *Modern Language Notes*, XLIV (1929), 159–160.

61. *Saison* is glossed "an Englishman" and *Saissonaëg* "English" in *The Breuiary of Britayne*, ed. Thomas Twyne, 1573, f. 96. The definitions of "Briton" in *Webster's Collegiate Dictionary*, 1925, show the way the wind has blown: "1. A member of one of the tribes inhabiting Britain before the Anglo-Saxon invasions. 2. A native, or British-born, subject of Great Britain, *esp. an Englishman*." The italics are mine.

62. *Edmund Spenser*, 1925, p. 15. Renwick refers to *The First Part Of The Elementarie VVhich Entreateth Chefelie Of The right writing of our English tung*. No second part was ever published.

63. *Positions Wherin Those Primitiue Circumstances Be Examined, Which Are Necessarie For The Training vp of children, either for skill in their booke, or health in their bodie* (two issues). See *DNB.* for doubtful references to other editions.

64. Issue with imprint "Thomas Vautrollier," pp. 101–102 (British Museum 1030. i. 10.).

65. *Elementarie*, 1582, sig. Hhᵛ.

66. Printed in William Wood's *Bow-mans Glory; or, Archery Revived*, 1682, pp. 33–67, and in T. Roberts' *English Bowman, or Tracts on Archery*, 1801, pp. 253–275.

67. T. Roberts, *The English Bowman*, 1801, p. 258.

68. The same, p. 86. The association of Arthur, the Round Table, and archery with the royal house is certainly as old as the Angevin dynasty. Champions in the rôle of Arthur's knights participated in jousts in the reigns of Henry III and Edward I. See Chambers, *Arthur of Britain*, pp. 127, 279–281. Edward III, whom Froissart reckons a king without his like "since the time of King Arthur who was aforetime King of England" (Sydney Armitage-Smith, *John of Gaunt*, 1904, p. 186), with the Black Prince, whom William Harbert would have to be "Great *Arthurs* heire" (*A Prophesie of Cad-*

wallader, 1604, sig. C2), according to Adam Murimuth, vowed in 1344 to reëstablish the Round Table to the number of at least three hundred knights. See Chambers, pp. 128, 282. John of Gaunt and Lionel of Antwerp were among the famous members, and it is but a step from the fame of English archery at Crécy and Poitiers to the association of archery with Arthur in the reign of Henry VII. Sir John Harington's remarks on Arthur are important in this connection: "He instituted an order of the knights of the round table onely (as it seems) of some meriment of hunting, or some pleasant exercises" (notes to *Orlando Furioso*, 1591, p. 29).

69. Roberts, *The English Bowman*, p. 258.

70. Rollins, *Analytical Index to the Ballad-Entries*, No. 1746, p. 151.

71. The same, No. 2265, pp. 195–196. See also No. 1329, p. 115.

72. Roberts, *The English Bowman*, p. 271.

73. The same, p. 268.

74. The same, p. 270.

75. This Richard Robinson (*fl.* 1576–1600), who generally styles himself "Citizen of London," is not to be confused with the poet Richard Robinson of Alton (*fl.* 1574), who is best known for *The rewarde of Wickednesse*, 1574, and *A Golden Mirrour*, 1589. The confusion is made by Haslewood in Brydges' *British Bibliographer*, I, 109 ff. On "Citizen" Robinson, hack-writer and member of the Leather-sellers Co., see *DNB.* and G. M. Vogt, "Richard Robinson's *Eupolemia* (1603)," *Studies in Philology*, XXI (1924), 629–648. In his *Eupolemia* (British Museum MS. Royal 18 A. lxvi, ff. 5–13) Robinson gives a bibliography of his works. A praise in MS. of Elizabeth, "Emanuel Elizabeta Dei Gratia," signed "By me Ry Robinson," is to be found in J. Bagford's *Collection for the History of Printing* (British Museum Harl. 5927.55.), f. 16ᵛ. That this Robinson was the father of Richard Robinson, an actor in Shakspere's plays, is not supported by any evidence.

76. Ed. Mead, *Chinon of England*, etc. (Early English Text Society, Original Series, No. 165), 1925, pp. 1–90 (following *Chinon of England*). Haslewood remarks that Elizabeth prob-

ably was "well acquainted with" Robinson's works, observing that Farmer possessed a copy of *A Learned and True Assertion* "having the Royal arms on the binding" (*The British Bibliographer*, I, 111, note). See *DNB.* for the many items dedicated by Robinson to Elizabeth, to whom he spoke in person for monetary reward.

77. Robinson had already published in 1576 *Certain Selected Histories for christian Recreations*, the Latin original of which is doubtfully attributed to Leland. This translation, expanded and with altered title, ran through many editions by 1648.

78. G. M. Vogt, "Richard Robinson's *Eupolemia* (1603)," *Studies in Philology*, XXI (1924), 635.

79. Lord Grey set sail from Ireland on August 31, 1582. Robinson's book was entered in the Stationers' Register on June 7 (Arber, *Transcript*, 1875, II, 412).

80. In 1579 Robinson dedicated *The Reverend D. Philip Melanthon his prayers . . . with the prayers of other learned Germaynes* to the "Honorable vertuous and renowmed gent Mr. Philip Sydney Esq." Vogt, *Studies in Philology*, XXI (1924), 632.

81. Or Smythe (d. 1591). See *DNB.* and *CSPD.*, 1581–91, *passim.* Smith was Robert Laneham's "good old freend."

82. Sig. A2.

83. Sigg. A4^v–B.

84. Sig. B.

85. Text: double quotes before *set*.

86. "Prolusion of 'Prince Arthur, with his Knights of the Round Table,' exhibited [in 1587] before the Queen," from an early 17th century manuscript, printed in Nichols' *Progresses and Public Processions of Queen Elizabeth*, 2nd ed., 1823, II, 529–530. The brackets are Nichols'.

87. (British Museum G. 11,235.) Sir Sidney Lee in his article on Leland in *DNB.* mistakes this for Robinson's translation of Leland's *Assertio*. For an analysis of *The Auncient Order*, see that by Haslewood in Brydges' *British Bibliographer*, I, 125 ff. *The Auncient Order* is referred to in British Museum MS. Lansd. 865, f. 160. It is quoted in Meredith Hanmer's *Chronicle of Ireland*, ed. Ware, together with Spen-

ser's *View of Ireland*, etc., 1633, p. 51 (sig. Ee2). The date of "Prince Arthur's Societie by R. R., London, 1588," in *Catalogue MS. Abp. Tenison's Library, St. Martin in Fields*, no date, is a mistake for 1583. Archbishop Tenison's copy is bound up with *A Learned and True Assertion* in Lambeth Palace (London) 6.1.25.

88. Sig. B.

89. Brydges, *The British Bibliographer*, I, 125.

90. Vogt, *Studies in Philology*, XXI (1924), 636.

91. Paris, [1520?] (British Museum 607.a.24.). No 1546 edition seems to be in evidence. In British Museum MS. Lansd. 865, f. 161, begins an incomplete transcript of an edition by "Barbe Regnault . . . printed at Paris 1559. 12°." There are other editions: Anthoine Houic, Paris, [1585?] (British Museum 608.a.1.); Benoist Rigaud, Lyons, 1590 (British Museum 608.a.11.). Robinson's interest in the book evidently began "by conference with Master *Steuen Batman*, a learned Preacher and friendlie fauourer of vertue and learning," who had helped him in his translation of Leland's *Assertio* "touching the praise worthie progenie of this *K. Arthure.*" Robinson says that Batman "shewed me out of his auncient records the interchaunges of King *Arthures* armes." Robinson then "had intelligence of a certaine French booke . . . beeing in an English mans handes": the Englishman "willingly shewed it & lent it me." See *A Learned and True Assertion*, sigg. B3–B3ᵛ. Robert Chester refers to *La deuise* or to some other of the numerous French heraldic books of the time: "I my selfe haue seen imprinted, a french Pamphlet of the arms of king *Arthur*, and his renowmed valiant Knights, set in colours by the Heraulds of *France*" ("*The Birth, Life* and Death of honourable Arthur *King of Brittaine*," in *The Anuals* [*sic*] *of great Brittaine*, 1611, p. 35). See also William Camden, *Remaines concerning Britaine*, 1637, p. 342: "Childish it is to referre hither [*i. e.*, to the discussion of "Impreses"] the shields of King *Arthurs* round-table Knights, when they were devised, as it is probable, for no other end, but to teach yong men the termes of Blazon." In his *Eupolemia* Robinson lists "a rare, true and proper blazon of coloures in Armoryes and Ensignes mili-

tary." Of a proposed second edition he states: "In the yeare of our Lord 1599 I added a præface in the beginning, and a peroration or conclusion in the ending, and gave yt to the Capteynes of the City for theyr encoragem^t. agenst all inward & owteward Enemyes, wherof I keepe the originall written copy. In perpetuam rei memoriam. Vntill God enable mee to publish yt in printe" (Brydges, *The British Bibliographer*, I, 125–126).

92. For the list of knights, see *A Learned and True Assertion*, sigg. [B4]–[B4^v], and *The British Bibliographer*, I, 116–117, note. Robinson divides the list into 16 kings, 1 duke, and 149 knights, making a "Summa totalis" of "166. Knightes." But "52" is reckoned twice, and Robinson's total should be 167, a total still one less than the number in the copy of *La deuise* that I have used.

93. Sig. [A4^v].

94. Aside from economy's sake, Robinson had authority for making the change: Batman had shown him an escutcheon which contained "in a shield *Azure*, (blew) three c[r]ownes, *Or.* (gold.)" (*A Learned and True Assertion*, sig. B3^v). Cf. *Le Blason des Armoiries*, Lyons, 1581, sig. xij: "De Artus, qu'on dit auoir esté Roy de la grande Bretaigne, quelques vns on dit qu'il n'auoit que trois couronnes, les autres six, vn autre neuf, tantost mises en triangle maintenant en pal: & ainsi diuersement." Similar examples could be multiplied.

95. The names of the fifty-eight knights with their initials (sigg. B^v–I2) are as follows: (1) S. Lancelot du Lac. H. O.; (2) S. Boort de [Gannes]. H. K.; (3) S. Gowaine de Orcany. E. D.; (4) Messyr Tristran de Lyonis. G. T.; (5) Sir Lyonnet de [Gannes]. W. C.; (6) Helyas le Blanc. — H.; (7) Hector des Mares. W. O.; (8) Blyomberyes de [Gannes].—; (9) Messire Gaherryet. —; (10) Keux le seneschall. — ; (11) Messire Iuaine. — ; (12) Bruor le Noir. W. B.; (13) S. Segurades. T. T.; (14) S. Patris le Hardy. I. A.; (15) S. Saphar le Mescogneu. I. E.; (16) S. Sagremor le Desree. B. S.; (17) Le Roy Ban de Benock. I. W.; (18) Le Roy de Claris. T. H.; (19) Le Morhoult de Ireland. T. M.; (20) Danayn le Roux. I. L.; (21) S. Brallain, sirnamed, as ye would say: Le Cheuallier aux deux Espées. T.

C.; (22) Galehault. R. B.; (23) Lamorat de Listenoys. W. H.;
(24) Messire Gullat. W. D.; (25) S. Gueherries. M. C. B. s.;
(26) Aggrauain le Orguelleux. W. M.; (27) Dodynel le sauage.
W. D.; (28) Osement Coeur hardy. I. E.; (29) Mador de la
Port. N. G.; (30) Dynadem d'Estrangore. T. C.; (31) Eglan-
tine Rochemont. T. B.; (32) Guallogrenant de windesor. R.
B.; (33) Sir Brandelys. T. C.; (34) Sir Leonard le hardy. W.
B.; (35) Bruyant des Isles. T. B.; (36) Henry le Ioyeux. H. S.;
(37) Meliadus del Espinoy. I. B.; (38) Meliadus le Noir oeil.
I. R.; (39) Surados des sept Fountaines. I. W.; (40) Lucan le
Bouteiller. I. M.; (41) Persides le Gent. W. C.; (42) Tuscane
le Romane. T. P.; (43) Godfry le Lacois. I. P.; (44) Thor le
Filz de Arez. I. W.; (45) Perceual de Galles. W. A.; (46) Sadoc
de Vencon. I. N.; (47) Gringalois le Fort. W. R.; (48) Mala-
quin le Galoys. W. T.; (49) Talemor le Volant. I. R.; (50)
Arain du Pin. H. B.; (51) Messire Palamides. A. W.; (52) Sir
Hebis. W. B.; (53) S. Lamwell of Cardyff. E. P.; (54) S. Pheti-
pace of Winchelsey. T. C.; (55) S. Plaine de force. P. D.; (56)
S. Bodovier of Winchelsey. — ; (57) S. Degraine sans Mal. I.
P.; (58) S. Pryamus. T. H.

Since five sets of initials are missing from the list of fifty-
eight knights, and since Robinson himself found only fifty-six
knights with Thomas Smith at Mile End Green when he delivered the copies of *The Auncient Order*, the membership (or
the attendance) of the archery club was obviously not stabil-
ized. For lack of sufficient information, furthermore, even
though Mulcaster's testimony reveals the identity of Sir
Lancelot, we cannot be positive that the other members of the
organization actually bore the names of the knights which
Robinson assigns them. After all, Robinson was compiling for
shillings and pence, and he had before him the list of knights
in *La deuise*. Nevertheless, the unriddling of the initials will
add a curious fact to the lives of many minor Elizabethans.
For example, if the knightly names were not assigned wholly
at random, "G. T." (No. 4) looks suspiciously like George
Turbervile when we consider Turbervile's work with "olde
Trystrams booke." See *The Noble Arte of Venerie or Hunting*, 1575, sigg. C.iiij, [F.viij^v], P.v^v, and *passim*. What of

Thomas Churchyard in respect to Nos. 21, 30, and 33? But
Churchyard usually makes it a point to speak autobiograph-
ically whenever and wherever he can, and for once he is re-
grettably silent. The relation of Robinson and Churchyard is
shown by Churchyard's preface to *A True Discourse Historicall, of the Succeeding Gouernours in the Netherlands*, 1602,
where he states that owing to his illness Robinson did the bulk
of the translating, and Churchyard commends him as "a man
more debased by many then he merits of any, so good parts are
there in the man." Churchyard contributes "A Praise of the
Bovve and Commendation of this Booke" to *The Auncient
Order*, sigg. [*₊*3ᵛ]–[*₊*4ᵛ], signed "T. Churchyard."

96. Hugh Offley (or Offly, or Ofly, or Ofley, or Opheley),
half-brother to Sir Thomas Offley and son-in-law of Robert
Harding, was sheriff of London, together with Richard Salten-
stall, in the year of the Armada, during the mayoralties of Sir
Martin Calthrope and Richard Martin (John Stow, *A Suruay
of London*, 1598, p. 448). In 1589 Robert Greene dedicated to
him *The Spanish Masquerado* (two issues). On August 13,
1589, William Jones licensed the following broadside: "Dis-
crybinge the vallure of our Englishe Archers and shott that
accompanied the Black Prince of Portugall their governor into
the feildes on twesdaie the 12 of August with the welcome into
Lymestreete by master Hugh Offley." See Rollins, *Analytical
Index to the Ballad-Entries*, No. 540, p. 53. See also *CSPD.*,
1581–90, for more information about Offley.

97. Sig. Bᵛ. Cf. Brydges, *The British Bibliographer*, I, 128,
note. A merchant's mark in the central panel of the lid of a
fine inlaid chest which was given by Offley to St. Saviour's,
Southwark (now Southwark Cathedral), contains the initials
"H. H. O.," *i. e.*, Hugh Harding Offley.

98. Nos. 8, 9, 10, 11, and 56, sigg. C, Cᵛ, C2, C2ᵛ, and I,
respectively. Mulcaster has words "To the curteous Reader"
in Robinson's *Third Proceeding in the Harmonie of King
Dauids Harp*, 1595 (Bodleian Mason H. 133.3.), sig. [A. 4ᵛ].
The shield of No. 6, "Helyas le Blanc," is flanked by only one
initial: "H," to the right.

99. *2 Henry IV*, iii, 2 (Student's Cambridge *Shakespeare*,
p. 583). Sir Dagonet, "kynge Arthurs foole" in Malory's

Morte d'Arthur, who "att euery turnement . . . beganne to make Kynge Arthur to laughe" (ed. Sommer, I, 432), appears as one of the twenty-four "namyd Knyhtes" around the edge of the traditional Round Table at Winchester (Shore, "King Arthur and the Round Table at Winchester," p. 199). In Ben Jonson's *Every Man Out of His Humour*, iv, 4, Carlo exclaims at the approach of Sogliardo and Shift: "Ods so, look here, man; Sir Dagonet and his squire." The Citizen's words — "You are well read in histories. I pray you, what was Sir Dagonet?" — in Beaumont and Fletcher's *Knight of the Burning Pestle*, iv, imply that the general populace knew either Malory or some contemporary use of romance material in which Sir Dagonet appeared, or both. But even though Dagonet (applied sometimes to a fool or a coward as an epithet of contempt) is the tool of Shakspere's satire, nevertheless Shakspere refers to the archery club of Prince Arthur's knights as Edmond Malone first pointed out in 1790 (*The Plays and Poems of William Shakspeare*, 1790, V, 365, note 1, continued to p. 367). C. R. Baskervill states that "Robinson gives many details of the history of the Round Table as a disguising in England." "Some Evidence for Early Romantic Plays in England — Concluded," *Modern Philology*, XIV (1916–17), 478, note 2. Just how long the society of Prince Arthur's archer-knights continued in existence is not known. See Rollins, *Analytical Index to the Ballad-Entries*, Nos. 231 and 979, pp. 28 and 88, respectively, for two later broadsides which may or may not be related to it. Hugh Offley apparently succeeded Thomas Smith as Prince Arthur of the society, for printed in the margin of Richard Niccols' *Londons Artillery*, 1616 (British Museum 11631.aaa.25.), p. 88, as a note to "Londons Prince Arthur," we get "Opheley Sheriffe of London." The tradition of the prowess of English bowmen gave way to the new artillery very slowly, for in the time of Charles II "we find the fraternity of bowmen flourishing and rejoicing in the patronage of a queen." See *Bishop Percy's Folio Manuscript*, ed. Hales and Furnivall, 1867–69, I (1867), 9.

100. "De Antiquitate & origine Almae & Immaculatae Universitatis Cantebrigiae," ed. Hearne in *Thomae Sprotti Chron-*

ica, 1719, pp. 268–269: "Kynotum virum providum constitue-
rat rex Arthurus rectorem anno ab incarnacione Domini quin-
gentesimo vicesimo nono, cui rex concessit tale privilegium:
'Arthurus regali à Deo fretus dignitate omnibus servis salu-
tem.'" Then follows the supposed charter, at the conclusion of
which we find: "Scripta autem est cartula anno ab incarnacione Domini 531. septimo Aprilis in civitate Londoniensi.
Et pro ampliori firmitate rex Arthurus transmisit cartulam
praedictam Kynoto, rectori scolarium civitatis praedictae, per
suum nepotem Walwanum probitate clarum." Cantalupus
(p. 269) attributes to Mordred the decline of Cambridge "post
mortem incliti regis Arthuri": "Nefandi Ambrones, Picti, &
Saxones, quos proditor ille Modredus invitaverat, Christicolas
studentes pariter & cives Cantebr. gladiis & flammis, ut lupi
oves, exterminant, fertilem patriam orientis Britanniae de-
vastabant."

101. Or Key, or Keyes, or John Caius, Jr. (d. 1573). See
DNB.

102. Or Key, or Kaye (d. 1572). John and Thomas were not
lineally related.

103. First published by Hearne as "Animadversiones
Aliquot In Londinensis de Antiquitate Cantabrigiensis
Academiae Libros Duos," in *Thomae Caii . . . Vindiciae
Antiquitatis Academiae Oxoniensis*, 1730, II, [315]–437. The
"Animadversiones" was drawn upon by Brian Twyne in his
Antiquitatis Academiae Oxoniensis Apologia, 1608 (Bodleian
Seld. 4°. T. 22. Art.), on pp. 51 ff. of which Arthur's connection
with Cambridge is denied: "Arthurum restituisse Cantabrigiā,
falsū." See also ed. 1620 (Bodleian Gough Adds. Oxon.
8.271.). The controversy had various other ramifications.

104. *Assertio Antiquitatis Oxoniensis Academiae*, ed. 1574,
p. 1.

105. *De Antiquitate Cantebrigiensis Academiae*, ed. 1574
(British Museum 731. i. 2., a "duobus" issue), p. 50. See H. R.
Plomer, *The Library*, New Series, Vol. VII, No. 3 (1926), pp.
253–268.

106. The same, pp. 50–51.

107. The same, p. 52.

108. Henry of Marlborough, or Marleburrough (*fl.* 1420). See *DNB*.

109. *De Antiquitate Cantebrigiensis Academiae,* ed. 1574, pp. 53, 55.

110. "Animadversiones," ed. Hearne, 1730, II, 340.

111. Sig. E.

112. William Nicolson, *The English Historical Library,* [1696]–99, Part II, pp. 219–220.

113. *Works,* ed. Grosart, 1884, I, 128.

114. IV, xi, 34:7; 26:7. C. G. Osgood links up these words of Spenser with "the contest for seniority then raging between the two universities," but Osgood is not concerned with, and makes no mention of, the Arthurian legend. "Spenser's English Rivers," *Transactions of the Connecticut Academy of Arts and Sciences,* XXIII (1919–20), 82. For evidence that Spenser knew Caius's book in another connection, see *The Faerie Queene,* IV, xi, 35: 1–6, and Osgood, p. 83.

115. (British Museum 598.a.35.). The dedication to Abraham Ortelius, sigg. A2–A2ᵛ, is dated "30. Augusti, 1568."

116. *Commentarioli,* f. 19; *Breuiary,* f. 22: "infamous beggage groome." Lhuyd cast other asperions on Polydore: "vir perfrictae frontis," "os impudens" (*Commentarioli,* f. 19). See George Gordon, "The Trojans in Britain," *Essays and Studies by Members of the English Association,* IX (1924), 21, note 2.

117. *Breuiary,* ff. 90, 93ᵛ.

118. The same, f. 28ᵛ.

119. The same, ff. 6–6ᵛ.

120. The same, f. 6ᵛ.

121. The same, f. 90.

122. The same, f. 9ᵛ: "my freende *M. Leland.*"

123. Chambers, *Arthur of Britain,* pp. 128 ff.

124. *The Romance and Prophecies of Thomas of Erceldoune,* ed. James A. H. Murray (Early English Text Society, Original Series, No. 61), 1875, pp. xxvii–xxx, xxxvi–xxxvii. During the Scottish wars of the Edwards, and on down into the sixteenth century, the Scots found encouragement in the promise that the "kyd conquerour" would extirpate the Saxons. Before the days of the Tudors, of course, the Welsh thought of *Saxons*

as equivalent to *English* in a linguistic or ethnological sense, and, in turn, the Lowland Scots, who were also *Sasunnach* to the Welsh, extended *Saxons* to mean *English* in a political sense. *Ca.* 1549 the author of *The Complaynt of Scotlande* observes that "inglismen gifis ferme credit to diuerse prophane propheseis of merlyne, and til vthir ald corruppit vaticinaris," and he goes on to say that he hopes the prophecies will be fulfilled in a different way from that which the English expect. *The Complaynt of Scotlande*, ed. Murray (Early English Text Society, Extra Series, XVII–XVIII), 1872, pp. 82–83. For various prophecies in English relating to English kings, see Rupert Taylor, *The Political Prophecy in England*, 1911.

125. *A Declaration, Conteynyng the Iust Causes and consyderations, of this present warre with the Scottis*, 1542, sig. [Biiij]. From Edward I to Edward VI such doctrine was frequently called to the attention of the Scots. See, among other items, James Harryson, *An Exhortacion to the Scottes*, 1547; Protector Somerset, *An Epistle or exhortacion, to vnitie & peace*, 1548; and Nicholas Bodrugan, *An Epitome of the title that the Kynges Maiestie of Englande, hathe to the souereigntie of Scotlande*, 1548.

126. On Margaret Tudor's conduct as Queen of Scotland, see "Tudor Intrigues in Scotland," *Scottish Review*, XXIV (1894), 225–252.

127. Consider a letter from Robert Bowes to Lord Burghley, Edinburgh, November 12, 1596, and another from George Nicolson to Sir Robert Cecil, Edinburgh, February 25, 1598 (Carpenter, *Reference Guide*, pp. 41–42). According to Drummond of Hawthornden, Ben Jonson reported that "in that paper S. W. Raughly had of the Allegories of his Fayrie Queen, by the Blating Beast the Puritans were understood, by the false Duessa the Q. of Scots" (*Ben Jonson's Conversations with William Drummond of Hawthornden*, ed. R. F. Patterson, 1923, p. 17). Cf. Evelyn M. Albright, *Dramatic Publication in England, 1580–1640*, 1927, pp. 150–152.

128. Thomas Powell, *Welch Bayte to spare Prouender*, 1603, sigg. D3–E.

129. *Breuiary*, f. 38.

130. The same, ff. 91ᵛ–92. Lhuyd (f. 92ᵛ) also commends his cousins across the Channel: "Neither yet the *Brittons*, which dwell nigh *Fraunce*, a nation of the same broode, doo any whit degenerate from their forefathers." The "Gothus" cited by Lhuyd is probably Matthæus Gothus (*fl.* 1573).

131. The same, sigg. ¶ᵛ–¶ij.

132. *Gabriel Harvey's Marginalia*, ed. G. C. Moore Smith, 1913, p. 164.

133. *The Correspondence of Philip Sidney and Hubert Languet*, ed. Bradley, pp. 36–37.

134. The same, pp. 38–39.

135. The edition also contains Lhuyd's letter to Abraham Ortelius, April 5, 1568, entitled "De Mona Druidum Insula," sigg. Aa–Ccij. See also Price's *Britanniae Histor⁻ Defensio*, British Museum MS. Cotton Titus F. iii, ff. 170–216ᵛ. Wood (*Athenae Oxonienses*, ed. Bliss, I, 217) mentions Price's *Defensio Regis Arthuri* in manuscript.

136. Sigg. ¶. ijᵛ–¶. iij.

137. Sig. ¶. iij.

138. Pp. 109–140.

139. Pp. 141–160.

140. P. 109.

141. Sigg. H.ij–H.iii. See also the 2nd ed., "now increased and altered after the Authors owne last Copie," 1596, sigg. F2–F3ᵛ.

142. Sig. H.ij.

143. Sig. H.iii.

144. *Ibid.* Lambard's common sense is further shown in his *Dictionarium Angliae Topographicum & Historicum*, a manuscript of *ca.* 1577, ed. 1730, p. 57: "Suerly neyther is every thinge true, nor al thinges feigned, that are reported of *Arthur.*" Again (p. 385): "I my selfe dare affirme nothinge of *Arthure*, neyther will I disalow al that other Men write of him: Only this I will say, that his Discredit is cheifly wrought by suche as have most laboured to blase him; for instede of wynninge Credit to his Actes, they have gayned Shame of their owne Follies."

145. Powel says he had "two ancient copies" of Caradoc which he used for correction of Lhuyd's translation when necessary, as well as "another larger copie of the same translation, being better corrected, at the hands of Robert Glouer Somerset Herald." Attention should be called to John Taylor the Water Poet's epitome of Powel's edition: "*Cambria Brittania:* OR, *A short Abreviation of the History, and Chronicles of* WALES," in *A Short Relation of a Long Iourney Made Round or Ovall*, [1652], pp. [29]–48. Powel's compilation was generally known to the Elizabethans as "Dr. Powel's historie," and not Caradoc's or Lhuyd's, and it remained for long the standard history of Wales.

146. Sigg. A.j–[B.iij^v].

147. Sig. [¶.vij^v].

148. Sig. A.ij.

149. Sig. Ff.j.

150. Sig. A.2.

151. P. 40.

152. P. 37.

153. *The Breuiary of Britayne*, 1573, f. 50. If the testimony of Miss Hetty Jones (of Dowlais, Glamorganshire, South Wales), a Welsh maid in my lodgings in London for a greater part of 1929 and 1930, be considered true, the tradition has been preserved to the present day. According to Miss Jones, Northwallians speak the purer Welsh, bring their children up on it from the cradle, and look down on the decadent Welsh of the Southwallians. Northwallians, as a rule, dislike the English, whereas the Southwallians, owing to the degeneration of their old language, are ashamed to call themselves Welsh, and prefer to be considered English.

154. *Pontici Virunnii Viri Doctissimi Britannicae Historiae Libri Sex, Magna Et Fide Et Diligentia Conscripti: Ad Britannici codicis fidem correcti, & ab infinitis mendis liberati: quibus praefixus est catalogus Regum Britanniae.* In the catalogue of British kings from Brutus to Cadwalader, Arthur is said to have ascended the throne in 516 and to have reigned for twenty-six years. The edition also contains, with Powel's annotations and with a dedication to Sir Philip Sidney,

Giraldus Cambrensis' *Itinerarium Cambriae* and *Cambriae Descriptio*. The pagination is continuous. See *DNB*. for other editions of both items.

155. Sig. A3ᵛ.

156. Sig. A4.

157. Sigg. A4–A4ᵛ.

158. Printed marginal commentary, sig. A2ᵛ.

159. Sigg. C2, C3ᵛ–[C4].

160. Sigg. [D4ᵛ] ff.

161. (British Museum G. 5932.). The initials "R. H." appear on the title-page. The dedication, sigg. A2–A2ᵛ, is signed "Richard Haruey."

162. Grosart *Spenser*, IX, 66, 68, 76, 90, 93, 96.

163. The same, p. 90.

164. The same, pp. 68–69. In a letter to Thomas Randolph in 1572, Buchanan writes: "As to my occupation at thys present tyme, I am besy with our Story of Scotland, to purge it of sum Inglis lyis and Scottis vanite" (*Original Letters*, ed. Ellis, Third Series, 1846, III, 374). In the 1587 edition of Camden's *Britannia*, p. 7, he is listed as one of the deniers of the story of Brutus.

165. P. 32. The allusion was first pointed out in my article, "Spenser and the Arthurian Legend," *Review of English Studies*, VI (1930), 172.

166. Sig. A2ᵛ.

167. P. 12.

168. P. 1. The article on Harvey in *DNB*. gives the impression that Harvey calls Buchanan "the trumpet of *Scotland*." McKerrow corrects the error in *The Works of Thomas Nashe*, 1904–10, V (1910), 173.

169. P. 2.

170. Pp. 6–7.

171. Pp. 8–9, 13.

172. Pp. 4, 17, 97.

173. The concluding sentence of the book, p. 107.

174. Pp. 88–89.

175. Pp. 90–91. It is not an exaggeration to state that the literature of the Elizabethan age is replete with Arthurian al-

lusions, and they bob up betimes where they are least to be expected. Thomas Howell in his poem "A Dreame," in which he
states that he wastes no labor to climb "the high and hauty
hyll" of poetry, observes that "King ARTHVRS Knights long
since are fled" (H. His Deuises, 1581, ed. Raleigh, Tudor and
Stuart Library, I, 1906, p. 80). John Ferne's Blazon of Gentrie, 1586, Part II, p. 128, recounts an unusual story about
Thomas, Earl of Lancaster, whom Edward II found guilty of
treason: "He was scorned, and in derision, called King Arthure, and shortly after, he was condemned, and his head cut
off." Among other interesting allusions, attention is called to
the fame of Gawain's skull, which rivals that of Ben Jonson in
the seventeenth century. Malory narrates in the Morte d'Arthur (ed. Sommer, I, 843): "At the houre of none syr Gawayn
yelded vp the spyryte/ and thenne the kynge lete entiere hym
in a chappel within douer Castel/ and there yet alle men maye
see the sculle of hym/ and the same wound is sene that syr
Launcelot gaf hym in bataill/" Caxton repeats (Preface to the
Morte d'Arthur, 1485, ed. Sommer, I, 2): "Item in the castel of
douer ye may see Gauwayns skulle/" The "ossa p[a]ene Gi-
gantea" are among Leland's proofs in the Assertio, 1544, f. 7.
See also A Learned and True Assertion, 1582, sig. D3. By the
time of The Faerie Queene the skull has bounced into the
Nashe-Harvey offshoot of the Martin Marprelate controversy.
Nashe in the dedicatory epistle to Strange Newes, 1592
(Works, ed. McKerrow, I, 258), wishes: "O would thou hadst a
quaffing boule, which, like Gawens scull, should containe a
pecke, that thou mightst swappe off a hartie draught to the
successe of this voiage." Harvey replies in Pierces Supereroga-
tion, 1593 (Works, ed. Grosart, II, 129): "Other good fellowes
may tell Tales of Gawin: thou art Sir Gawin reuiued, or rather
Terrour in person. Yet shall I putt a beane into Gawins ratling
scull: and tell thee, where thy slashing Long-sword commeth
short?" And again (the same, pp. 237–238): "I . . . will en-
graue such an Epitaph, with such a Kyrieeleson vpon thy scull,
as shall make the remembred, when Syr Gawins scull shall be
forgotten." See Nashe's Works, ed. McKerrow, IV, 157, for
further references, and add Chester, Anuals [sic], 1611, p. 35.

176. There are also in manuscript many anonymous six-teenth-century attacks on "enemies" to the ancient British history. See, for example, British Museum MS. Cotton Titus F. iii, ff. 217 ff.

177. Sig. ¶ij. See also ed. 1601, sig. Aij.

178. Juan Luis Vives, or Ludovicus Vives (1492–1540), Spanish divine and sometime tutor of Mary I. Vives' attitude toward Arthurian romance, like that of Erasmus, is too well known for comment. For suggestions of his attitude toward the ancient British history, see John Twyne's De Rebus Al-bionicis, Britannicis atque Anglicis, ed. Thomas Twyne, 1590, passim.

179. Jean Bodin (ca. 1530–1596), French political writer. Bodin's mere quoting of Polydore for the British history would be sufficient to arouse the ire of loyal Britons. See I. Bodini Advocati Methodus, ad Facilem Historiarum Cognitionem, Paris, 1566 (British Museum 580.g.2.), pp. 314, 423.

180. John of Whethamstede, or Johannes Frumentarius (d. 1465), of whom R. H. Fletcher states: "I cannot find any-thing to that effect in the editions of Whethamstede's Regis-trum Abbatiae by Hearne and by Riley (Rolls Series, 1872)" (The Arthurian Material in the Chronicles, p. 182, note 4). But Whethamstede was skeptical of the British history, and the skeptical passage is quoted by Camden in the Britannia, 1586, pp. 6–7: "Inter quos [who doubt the ancient British his-tory] vnus Iohannes de Wheathamstead, abbas S. Albani, vir summi iudicij, instar omnium erit, qui olim hac de re in suo Granario sic scripsit." Then follows the pertinent passage, a part of which states that "totus processus de Bruto isto, poeticus est, potiùs quàm historicus." Camden quotes from Whethamstede's Granarium.

181. Hadrian Junius (1512–1575), Dutch physician, scholar, and emblem-writer, first added along with George Buchanan to the 1587 ed., p. 7.

182. Added along with William of Newburgh to the 1600 ed., pp. 7–8. Boccaccio's skepticism of Brutus was noticed by John Bale in 1549. See pp. 33 and 162, note 93, above.

183. To the 1607 ed., pp. 5–6, the following are added:
Giraldus Cambrensis; Nicolas Vignier the Elder (1530–1596),
French physician and historian (see his *Sommaire de l'Histoire des Francois*, Paris, 1579, and *Bibliothèque Historiale*,
1588); Gilbert Génébrard (1537–1597), Archbishop of Aix
and historian (see *Chronographia in duos libros distincta*,
Paris, 1567, the second book of which is by Arnauld de Pontac:
in the second book Polydore Vergil is frequently cited for
authority, and on sig. [N4ᵛ] he is listed among "historici cele-
bres"); "Molinæus," or Charles Du Moulin (1500–1566),
French jurisconsult (see his "De Origine, Progressu et Prae-
stantia Monarchiae regniq; Francorum," from the French
text of 1561, in *Monarchia S. Romani Imperii, siue Tractatus*,
ed. Melchior Goldast, Hanover and Frankfort, 1611–1614,
III, Frankfort, 1613, 45–66: on p. 48 the English story of
Brutus is dubbed "fabulosa," and on p. 49 Geoffrey of Monmouth is classed among writers "inertes illi rhapsodi").
Camden names William of Newburgh and Giraldus Cambrensis specifically as discreditors of Geoffrey of Monmouth,
and the others as deniers of the story of Brutus. In the 1594
edition, pp. 6–7, he states of Brutus: "Ego verò vt eiusmodi
virum huc aduenisse non negem, nomē tamen regioni indidisse
cum Humfredo Lhuiddo non affirmem." This reference to
Lhuyd is repeated in the 1600 edition, pp. 7–8, but is dropped
from the 1607 edition, pp. 5–6, and does not appear in the 1610
edition (the first English translation, by Philemon Holland).
To those who think Brutus the father and founder of Britain,
Camden states: "I will not be of a contrarie minde." Cf.
Aylett Sammes, *Britannia Antiqua Illustrata*, 1676, p. 161.

184. Sig. ¶2.

185. Sigg. ¶2–¶2ᵛ.

186. Pp. 6–7 (sigg. A3ᵛ–A4).

187. P. 7.

188. *Ibid.*

189. *The History of Great Britaine*, 1611, p. 164. See also
pp. 155 ff. The *History* was prepared as a continuation of *The
Theatre of the Empire of Great Britaine*, 1611–12, and the
pagination, with some irregularity, is continuous.

190. "From the Author of the Illustrations," sig. A2.

191. The same, sig. A2ᵛ.

192. Grosart *Spenser*, IX, 65.

193. The same, p. 78.

194. "Spenser Apocrypha," in *The Manly Anniversary Studies in Language and Literature*, 1923, pp. 64–69.

195. Sig. [F2]. The account of Brutus occupies sigg. A2–A2ᵛ: "BRutus Troianus, patria sua capta atq; deleta, naues ex longo errore ad hanc appulisse terram fertur, regnoque occupato sedem hîc nouae Reip. constituisse: eandam legibus atque institutis Troianis deuinxisse, ac nomine suo Britanniam nuncupasse, cùm ante id tempus Albion ei nomen fuisset. Brutus igitur regnum in hac Insula princeps obtinuit. Idem amplissimae antiquissimaeque ciuitatis, quam nunc Londinum vocamus, fundamenta iecit, eamq; nouo nomine Troinouantū (Caesar autem Trinobantum dicit) nominauit. Cum res Britanniae constituisset, quatuorque & viginti annos regnasset, Brutus è vita migrauit." Arthur appears under "*A. C.*/ 589.," sigg. B2ᵛ–B3: "QVo tempore etiam Arthurus Vtri filius 15. omnino annos natus suscepit Rempublicam, patriamque in liberanda patria gloriam multùm cumulauit. Is vndenorum annorum spatio, quo regnum Britanniae tenebat, duodenis maximis contra Saxones praelijs vsque superior fuit, eorumque opes & neruos vehemēter deminuit atque infirmauit: quos penitus ex Insula forsan expulisset, si non illius impetus & conatus mors in medio cursu immatura fregisset. Hoc lumine extincto, posteri non modo nihil acquirere, sed ne illa quidem, quae à maioribus accepissent, retinere potuerunt. Nunc enim Britanni in antiquam recidunt fortunam, eunt retro quotidiè, quoad continuis belli offensionibus propè consumpti solum tandem vertere, ac derelicta in perpetuum patria imperium dimittere, in Cambriamque rursus fuga se recipere compulsi sunt, neque post id tempus Britanni, sed ab Saxonibus Oualli (quae vox peregrinum illorum lingua valet) appellantur: Hi verò imperio potito, eoq; in 7. regna diuiso, totam eam terram, quam obtinebant, Angliam ab Anglis suis nuncuparunt."

196. *Manly Anniversary Studies*, p. 65. See also Carpenter's *Reference Guide*, p. 132. The British Museum Catalogue

assigns the conjectural date of 1570. Another edition of the chronicle came out in Hamburg in 1598.

197. *Ben Jonson's Conversations with William Drummond of Hawthornden*, ed. Patterson, p. 14.

198. Oxford *Spenser*, p. 473.

199. "The Matter of Britain," *Times Literary Supplement*, London, Thursday, November 14, 1929, p. 906.

200. Translated from the Latin manuscript by George Ridpath, 1695, pp. 20, 181. Craig's theme is whether Scotland owes homage to England, and he wishes especially to "revenge upon *Holinshed* the Injury done to our *Boethius* by *Leland*" (p. 430). His repudiation of Geoffrey and Geoffrey's Arthur is in no uncertain terms: "The sole Author of all this Fable of *Arthur*, is *Geffrey* of *Monmouth*, ... who is also sir-named *Arthur*, because he spread a Latin Vail over the Fictions of the Brittons concerning *Arthur*, which he hath augmented himself, and given them the name of True History. . . . Let *Arthur* then, with his Historian *Geffrey*, go and keep Company with the Night-Owls" (pp. 113, 114, 116).

201. The same, p. 44.

202. The same, p. 110.

203. Manuscript notes "of the end of the sixteenth or beginning of the seventeenth centuries," contributed by C. Hopper to *Notes and Queries*, Second Series, Vol. IV, No. 82 (1857), p. 67. It is not audaciously assumed for a moment that every defence of Geoffrey and every condemnation of Polydore in Spenser's day have been referred to, but sufficient evidence has been marshalled to show a clear-cut and decisive movement. For Thomas Stapleton's praise of Polydore, see his *Principiorum Fidei Doctrinalium Demonstratio Methodica*, ed. 1582 (cf. Henry Wharton, *Anglia Sacra*, 1691, Part I, p. xiv). John Foxe subscribes to the rumor that Polydore "pyled hys bokes together & set them all on a lyght fire" (*The Second Volume of the Ecclesiasticall History*, ed. 1576, p. 1116). John Caius adds to the rumor by specifying "histories" and "manuscripts," as many as "ne plaustrum quidem posset capere atque sustinere" (*De Antiquitate Cantebrigiensis Academiae*, ed. 1574, p. 52). Thomas Gale's report changes the "wagon

load" of Caius to a "ship load" (Preface to his *Historiae . . . Scriptores XV*, 1691, sig. *a*ᵛ). In his *Hypercritica, ca.* 1618, Edmund Bolton gives a Tudor "Muster of Names" in favor of Geoffrey of Monmouth against the ranks of Polydore: "*Leland* most famous, *Sr John Prise*, Knight, *Humfrey Lhuid*, &c., Men singularly skill'd in our Antiquities, and *Britanns* of Race, Doctor *Keyes*, Founder of Keyes College in *Cambridge*, Mr *Lambert* of Lincolns Inn . . ., Doctor *Powel*, Mr [John] *Lewis*, and all Welsh Bards and Genealogist's, Doctor [Richard] *White* of *Basingstoke* [see *DNB*.] in his Latin Histories, *Stowe*, *Holinshead*, &c. So that if the cause were to be try'd or carry'd by Voices, the affirmative would have the fuller Cry" (*Critical Essays of the Seventeenth Century*, ed. Spingarn, 1908, I, 87). See p. 199, note 29, below.

204. *The Breuiary of Britayne*, ff. 59ᵛ–60ᵛ.

205. The same, f. 7.

206. Quoted in illustration of Letter CC. in *Original Letters*, ed. Ellis, Second Series, 1827, III, 49.

207. Last stanza of *Britaines Honour. In the two Valiant Welchmen, who fought against fifteene thousand Scots, at their now comming to England passing over Tyne*, no date (Bodleian Wood 401.).

208. *The Welsh-Monster: or, the Rise and Downfal of that late Upstart, the R—t H—ble Innuendo Scribble*, [1708], p. 4.

209. *Henry V*, iv, 7, and v, 1.

210. Cf. Winstanley, *Aberystwyth Studies*, IV (1922), 64 ff.

211. Ed. Herbert S. Murch (*Yale Studies in English*, XXXIII), 1908, i, p. 23.

212. The same, iv, p. 73.

213. The same, ii, p. 32.

214. The same, iv, p. 75.

215. Maynadier points out that many of the subscribers to an 1812 edition of Thomas Heywood's *Life of Merlin, Sirnamed Ambrosius*, 1641, were "tradespeople of the lower classes: shoemakers, hairdressers, dressmakers, plasterers, and the like" (*The Arthur of the English Poets*, p. 291, note 1). Cf. a few Welsh proper names, ranging in date from 1603 to 1623, chosen from the *Calendar of Wynn (of Gwydir) Papers, 1515–*

1690, ed. [Ballinger], 1926: "Elliwe verch Cadwaladr," "Cadwaladr ap Jevan Wynn," "Cadwalader Tydir," "Owen Arthur," and "Mr. Cadwaladr the barber, near the White Hart in Holborn."

216. *A Letter: Whearin, part of the entertainment vntoo the Queenz Maiesty, at Killingwoorth Castl, in Warwik Shéer in this Soomerz Progress 1575.* iz *signified*, [1575], ed. Furnivall, *Captain Cox, His Ballads and Books; or, Robert Laneham's Letter* (Ballad Society, No. 7), 1871.

217. *The Complete Works of George Gascoigne*, ed. John W. Cunliffe, Cambridge English Classics, 1907–10, II (1910), 91–131. No copy of the first edition seems to be preserved. The reprint, "The Princely Pleasures at Kenelworth Castle," is from the text of 1587.

218. The same, p. 92. See Greenlaw, "Spenser's Fairy Mythology," *Studies in Philology*, XV (1918), 105 ff.

219. See C. R. Baskervill, "The Genesis of Spenser's Queen of Faerie," *Modern Philology*, XVIII (1920–21), 51.

CHAPTER IV

1. *Edmund Spenser*, p. 50. Professor Renwick's valuable study (hereafter referred to in this immediate section as Renwick) is vital for a comprehension of what Spenser was about. Professor Renwick renders into English all his quotations from other languages. The original is given here in each case, and thorough acknowledgment is made to Professor Renwick, not only for the spirit of his entire essay, but also, wherever necessary, for specific points. There is no need to quibble over whether Spenser was familiar with the contemporary literary criticism. See also M. Y. Hughes, "Virgil and Spenser," *University of California Publications in English*, II (1929), 263–418.

2. P. 193.

3. Ed. Henri Chamard, Paris, 1904, p. 233.

4. Marginalia in Thomas Twyne's English version, *The Surueye of the World*, 1572, of Dionysius Periegetes' *De Situ Orbis* (*Gabriel Harvey's Marginalia*, ed. G. C. Moore Smith, pp. 160–161; quoted in part by Renwick, p. 138).

5. The same, p. 161; Renwick, *ibid.*

6. The same, p. 162; Renwick, *ibid.*

7. *Letter-Book of Gabriel Harvey, A.D. 1573–1580*, ed. Edward J. L. Scott (Camden Society, New Series, XXIII), 1884 pp. 134–135; quoted in part by Renwick, *ibid.*

8. The same, p. 97.

9. Grosart *Spenser*, IX, 68.

10. "To the Reader," sig. [¶.vij^v].

11. Lady Violet Paget suggests such a point of view on Spenser's part, though she does not voice it in so many words (Vernon Lee, *Euphorion*, 1884, II, 112–118). Chambers' assertion that Spenser's revival of romance is an archaism does not conflict with the *speculum* idea (*The Mediaeval Stage*, 1903, I, 69). Thorough acknowledgment is made to Professor Edwin Greenlaw for his discussion of the idea in a class lecture, just as acknowledgment was made in my typewritten Master's thesis, *Antiquarianism in Edmund Spenser*, 1923, which is deposited in the library of the University of North Carolina, Chapel Hill, North Carolina.

12. *Gabriel Harvey's Marginalia*, ed. Smith, p. 164.

13. Renwick, p. 61.

14. Grosart *Spenser*, IX, 79. See also G. A. Thompson, "Poetry and Learning," in *Elizabethan Criticism of Poetry*, 1914, pp. 48–55.

15. *La Deffence*, ed. Chamard, pp. 233 ff.

16. The same, pp. 235–236; Renwick, p. 47.

17. Renwick, p. 45.

18. "Au Lecteur," prefaced to *La Franciade* in *Oeuvres Complètes de P. de Ronsard*, ed. Prosper Blanchemain, 1857–67, III (1858), 8.

19. *Oeuvres*, III, 23; Renwick, p. 48. As Renwick observes, the lateness of the date does not affect the significance of the trend of critical theory.

20. *Discorsi dei Romanzi*, Venice, 1554, pp. 11–12; Renwick, p. 51.

21. *I Romanzi*, Venice, 1554, pp. 25–26; Renwick, *ibid.* The similarity of Pigna's and Giraldi Cinthio's conclusions is striking. As Renwick observes, each accused the other of plagiarism.

22. Renwick, pp. 43–44.

23. The October eclogue of *The Shepheardes Calender*, line 59, Oxford *Spenser*, p. 457.

24. Sélincourt, Introduction to the Oxford *Spenser*, p. xli.

25. Lines 37–48, Oxford *Spenser*, p. 457.

26. The same, p. 458.

27. The same, p. 628.

28. *I Romanzi*, p. 48.

29. Henry Morley notes that "Turbervile's Arguments to Mantuan's eclogues are in the form resembling that which Spenser afterwards used" in the arguments to the cantos of *The Faerie Queene* (*English Writers*, IX, 33). Turbervile may well have set the type, though only one of Turbervile's arguments is in resolved riming septenaries, the form that Spenser uses. Morley quotes several examples of Turbervile's arguments, but in making the point does not quote the appropriate one. "The .vj. Egloge entituled CORNIX" shows "The Argument" in question:

> HOwe Countrey differs from the Towne
>   here Cornix he recites:
> He girdes the foolish sotted Sectes,
>   and gainst the witlesse writes.

See *The Eglogs of the Poet B. Mantuan Carmelitan, Turned into English Verse, & set forth with the Argument to euery Egloge by George Turbervile Gent.*, 1567 (British Museum 238.1.17.), sig. H.iiij.

30. Renwick, p. 52.

31. *An Aunswere to the Treatise of the Crosse*, 1565, f. 126^v.

32. *The chronicle of Ihon Hardyng*, 1543, sig. [i.vi^v]. Cf. Henry VII's twelve knights bannerets, who are frequently referred to.

33. Letter to Ralegh, Oxford *Spenser*, p. [407].

34. Shore, "King Arthur and the Round Table at Winchester," p. 199. See also Julian del Castillo, *Historia de los Reyes Godos*, Madrid, 1624, p. 365, and the triad *Arthur Ai Varchogion* ("Arthur and His Knights"), which pictures Arthur the chief knight over twenty-four other knights representing

specific qualities (Dwnn, *Tair Sir Deheubarth*, etc., 1586–1613, ed. Meyrick, 1846, I, 10).

35. Cf. J. D. Bruce, *The Evolution of Arthurian Romance*, 2nd ed., 1928, II, 40.

36. Cf. Sélincourt, Introduction to the Oxford *Spenser*, pp. xlii–xliii.

37. Cf. Sir John Harington's "Apologie of Poetrie," prefixed to *Orlando Furioso*, 1591, sig. [¶ vi^v]: "*Virgill* extolled *Æneas* to please *Augustus*, of whose race he was thought to come. *Ariosto* prayseth *Rogero* to the honour of the house of *Este*. *Æneas* hath his *Dido* that retaineth him, *Rogero* hath his *Alcina*." The Angevin dynasty had received its praise from Wolfram von Eschenbach, who connected the hero of *Parzival* with the House of "Anschowe," though some hold that Wolfram was but following his so-called source "Kiot," or "Kyot," which W. J. Entwistle links vaguely with Eleanor, daughter of Henry II and Eleanor of Aquitaine and wife of Alfonso VIII of Castile (*The Arthurian Legend in the Literatures of the Spanish Peninsula*, 1925, p. 33). Bruce considers that Wolfram's connection with the Austrian branch of the family in the province of Steiermark was "responsible for his fancy of making his hero belong to the world-famous house of the same name" (*The Evolution of Arthurian Romance*, I, 321, and notes 15 and 16). Tristram also was connected with the House of Anjou. See R. S. Loomis, "Tristram and the House of Anjou," *Modern Language Review*, XVII (1922), 24–30. The House of Bouillon was connected with the *Chevalier au Cygne*, and early in the sixteenth century, "at thinstygacion of the Puyssaunt & Ilustryous Prynce Lorde Edwarde Duke of Buckyngham," Robert Copland made an English translation as the "Hystory . . ., named Helyas the knight of the swanne of whom linially is dyscended my sayde Lorde" (*The Knight of the Swanne*, [1550?], ed. William Copland, sig. [A.i^v]). In his Latin prose condensation of Geoffrey of Monmouth's *Historia* (ed. David Powel, 1585), Ponticus Virunnius adds that from Bedver's son is descended the Venetian family of "Beduara" for whom he writes the book. Cf. Fletcher, *The Arthurian Material in the Chronicles*, 1906, p. 240.

38. Oxford *Spenser*, p. 628.

39. William Slatyer, "Lauro, ac Laude Dignis," in *Palae-Albion. The History of Great Britanie from the first peopling of this Iland to this presant Raigne of o' hapy and peacefull Monarke K. Iames*, 1621 (Bodleian M. 5. 6. Art.), sig. ¶¶ᵛ. In Slatyer's poem Chaucer, Sidney, "Iohnson," Drayton, Daniel, and others are praised together with "Spencer." This allusion to Spenser has not heretofore been pointed out.

40. "All the chief Old French Arthurian romances in prose were accessible at the library of the princes of Este in Ferrara in the fifteenth and sixteenth centuries." *Palamades* was Ariosto's favorite Arthurian romance, "next *Tristan*, thirdly, *longo intervallo, Lancelot*" (Bruce, *The Evolution of Arthurian Romance*, II, 25, notes 11 and 13).

41. *An Apologie for Poetrie*, ed. Arber, English Reprints, 1868, p. 55.

42. "Spenser and Sidney," *Anglia*, XXXVIII (1914), 191. See also Thompson, "The Appeal to Patriotism," in *Elizabethan Criticism of Poetry*, pp. 41–43.

43. *Ben Jonson's Conversations with William Drummond of Hawthornden*, ed. Patterson, p. 14.

44. *Works*, ed. Cunliffe, II, 93.

45. The same, pp. 93–94.

46. "The Critical Background of the Spenserian Stanza," *Modern Philology*, XXIV (1926–27), 36 and note 1. Miss Pope stresses "the inherent unity of Spenser's verse," and attempts to derive Spenser's stanza from a nine-line Italian madrigal.

47. "The Elizabethan Period: Poetry and Prose," *The Year's Work in English Studies*, VII (1926), 161.

48. "Spenser's Fairy Mythology," *Studies in Philology*, XV (1918), 106. Spenser's old schoolmaster, Richard Mulcaster, contributed to the entertainment Latin verses in praise of Elizabeth "which were expounded by an Actor clad like a Poet" (Gascoigne, *Works*, ed. Cunliffe, II, 95). "Perhaps" Mulcaster too was present: "perhaps" teacher and pupil met again in the Arthurian atmosphere!

49. Oxford *Spenser*, p. 422.

50. See Carpenter's *Reference Guide*, p. 85; Gabriel Harvey's *Works*, ed. Grosart, I, 180; and the Oxford *Spenser*, p. 463. Gascoigne died in 1577.

51. *La Deffence*, ed. Chamard, pp. 257–258. "The different attitude of Spenser is to some extent explained by the antiquarian tastes so widespread in England at the time" (Legouis, *Spenser*, 1926, p. 57).

52. *Oeuvres*, ed. Blanchemain, III, 36.

53. The same, VII, 320.

54. Oxford *Spenser*, p. [416].

55. Ed. Arber, English Reprints, 1869, p. 63; Renwick, p. 76.

56. *Spenser*, 1926, p. 57.

57. Sélincourt, Introduction to the Oxford *Spenser*, p. lxi.

58. Maurice Kyffin, *The Blessednes of Brytaine*, 1587, sig. [B4].

59. Pigna, *I Romanzi*, p. 21.

60. Bruce pronounces the *Avarchide* an "innovation — the most audacious, perhaps, in European literature" (*The Evolution of Arthurian Romance*, II, 40).

61. *Works*, ed. Cunliffe, II, 102.

62. Ed. *Chinon of England*, etc. (Early English Text Society, Original Series, No. 165), 1925, pp. xxxi–xxxii.

63. Renwick, p. 145.

64. Richard Robinson, *The Auncient Order*, 1583, sig. L 4.

65. Glosses to the April and June eclogues, Oxford *Spenser*, pp. 434, 443, respectively.

66. Miss Winstanley is of the belief that Ascham in *The Scholemaster* probably influenced Spenser's moral tone, and that Ascham also probably "dissuaded or helped to dissuade Spenser from making much use of Malory's *Morte d'Arthure*" (ed. *The Faerie Queene*, Book I, 1915, p. lxviii). But the more wholesome observation to make is that mediæval romance was objected to during the English Renaissance from at least three points of view: as an inspiration for immorality, as the work of papists, and as a poor criterion of literary form. In the list of objectors from one point of view or another, in addition to Ascham, are numbered Erasmus, Vives, Richard Hyrde,

Thomas Paynell, William Tyndale, Thomas Niccols, Thomas Underdown, Edward Dering, Thomas Bowes, Thomas Beard, Thomas Nashe, Sir William Cornwallis, Robert Ashley, Ben Jonson, and others. See R. S. Crane, *The Vogue of Medieval Chivalric Romance during the English Renaissance*, 1919, and "The Reading of an Elizabethan Youth," *Modern Philology*, XI (1913–14), 269–271.

67. *Spenser*, 1926, p. 34. See also "The Poets' Poet," *Times Literary Supplement*, London, Thursday, February 27, 1930, pp. [149]–150.

68. *An Apologie for Poetrie*, ed. Arber, p. 41.

69. *Ben Jonson's Conversations with William Drummond of Hawthornden*, ed. Patterson, p. 14.

70. Professor Berdan follows Schick's pedigree of certain features of Spenser's allegory: Martianus Capella — *Anticlaudianus — Court of Sapience — Pastime of Pleasure — Faerie Queene*. See J. Schick, *Lydgate's Temple of Glas* (Early English Text Society, Extra Series, LX), 1891, p. cxliv and note 1, and Berdan, *Early Tudor Poetry*, 1920, p. 92.

71. *Faerie Queene*, V, xi (Berdan's footnote 1, *Early Tudor Poetry*, p. 116).

72. *Early Tudor Poetry*, pp. 115–116.

73. Ed. 1567, f. 74. The edition of 1553 is incomplete, but the part quoted is the same. See also the triad *Arthur Ai Varchogion* ("Arthur and His Knights"), which pictures Arthur the chief knight over twenty-four other knights of specific characteristics: "PEDWAR Marchog ar hugaint o Varchogion urddolion oeddynt ynhy Arthyr yn wastad yn trigaw, a chyneddf orchestol oedd ar bob un o naddyn ar naill du ragor eraill." ("Four and twenty dignified knights always dwelt in the house of Arthur, each of whom possessed a peculiar eminent quality different from the others.") Then follow the knights by threes: "golden-tongued"; "chaste"; "of battle"; "who possessed the power of illusion"; "royal"; "just"; "of repugnance"; "counselling." "A thrwy i arfau kyssegredig ir oedd Arthur yn gorfod pob peth." ("And with his sacred arms Arthur overcame every thing.") (Dwnn, *Tair Sir Deheubarth*, etc., 1586–1613, ed. Meyrick, 1846, I, 10). The translation is the editor's.

The manuscript is addressed to Elizabeth, and, interestingly enough, the editor can see no reason why Dwnn prefaced his work with the triad. On the whole, the English literary critics of the Tudor period have little to say about the Arthurian legend. The author of *The Arte of English Poesie*, 1589, who is doubtfully considered to be George Puttenham, defends the "short historicall ditty" and says that he has written "a litle brief *Romance* or historicall ditty in the English tong of the Isle of great *Britaine* in short and long meetres, and by breaches or diuisions to be more commodiously song to the harpe in places of assembly, where the company shalbe desirous to hear of old aduentures and valiaunces of noble knights in times past, as are those of king *Arthur* and his knights of the round table, Sir *Beuys* of *Southampton*, *Guy* of *Warvvicke*, and others like" (ed. Arber, English Reprints, 1869, p. 57).

74. Pigna, *I Romanzi*, p. 26.

75. Robinson, *A Learned and True Assertion*, sig. A2.

76. Spenser's Letter to Ralegh, Oxford *Spenser*, p. [407].

77. See Nichols' *Progresses and Public Processions of Queen Elizabeth*, 2nd ed., 1823, II, 529–530, and pp. 60–61, above.

CHAPTER V

1. Murray points out that the prophecy of the "French wife's son" in "The prophecie of Bertlington," which failed in its original application to John, Duke of Albany, found its way into the 1603 "Prophecie of Thomas Rymour." Mary Queen of Scots became the "French wife," and when the "son" became King of England, Thomas received acclaim as author of the prophecy. Murray states that "the fame of Thomas Rymour gradually outshone all of his rivals, so that his pretended sayings were interpolated, and even his authority quoted, to give greater authority to theirs." See *The Romance and Prophecies of Thomas of Erceldoune* (Early English Text Society, Original Series, No. 61), 1875, pp. xxvii–xxx, xxxvi–xxxvii. For various prophecies supposed to have been fulfilled by the accession of James, see *The Whole Prophecies of Scot-*

land, England, France, Ireland and Denmarke, ed. Edinburgh, 1617. For various points in the problem of succession involving the Trojan and Arthurian legends, see A. E. Parsons, "The Trojan Legend in England," *Modern Language Review,* XXIV (1929), 399 ff. For a variant of the "HEMPE" prophecy "*conferd on* Merlin," see Thomas Heywood, *The Life of Merlin,* 1641, p. 361.

2. Sig. B.

3. Sig. B^v.

4. Sig. B3^v.

5. Queen's College (Oxford) MS. $\frac{D.13}{43}$, which is in Harry's own hand:

THE/ WELLSPRINGE/ of true nobilitie/ *yeldinge foorth an ocean of Heroicall descentes & Roiall/ genealogies of the renoumed Kinges Princes greate/* states nobilitie and gentrie of this famouse/ Ile of Brittaine descended of the bloud/ Royall of the auntient Brittaynes But/ pricipallye the Genealogie of the/ *most highe & mightie Monarche/ our dread Soueraigne Iames/* By the grace of God kinge of greate Brittayne France/ *and Irelande de/ fender of the faithe/ &c/* With manye other matters worthie of note/ *Gathered by George Owen/ Harrye Rector of Whitchurch/ in Kemes/ Blessed is that lande whose King is descended/ of nobles* Eccle: 10:/ The Contentes of the whole book you shall finde/ in the next pag: [*sic*]

The manuscript (of about 300 pages) is much more extensive than Harry's published work, as it includes genealogies of the nobility and of foreign kings. The principal genealogy in both begins with Noah. The name of Prince Henry is added to the manuscript on page 89. Many corrections and additions are pasted in, all of which are seemingly in the same hand.

6. Pp. 39–40; *The Wellspringe of true nobilitie,* pp. 71–72.

7. Ed. 1600, sig. [G5^v]. The issues vary.

8. Henry Chettle (?), *Englandes Mourning Garment: Worne here by plaine Shepheardes; in memorie of their sacred Mistresse, Elizabeth,* no date, sig. [A4^v].

9. Maurice Kyffin, *A Defence of the Honourable sentence and execution of the Queene of Scots, ca.* 1587, sig. D2.

10. Joseph Hunter states: "There is something remarkable in the King preferring to trace his descent from Henry VII. and Elizabeth of York, through his *father* rather than his *mother*; and to exhibit so obscurely that his great-grandmother was also Queen of Scotland." "Heraldry of the Monument of Queen Elizabeth, at Westminster," *Archaeologia Cambrensis*, New Series, I (1850), 199.

11. For the very interesting connection of this independent claim with Shakspere's *Macbeth*, see Parsons, "The Trojan Legend in England," *Modern Language Review*, XXIV (1929), 404 ff. It should be kept in mind that the Scots had never consented to the English point of view of the supremacy of the whole island. Through the work of the Scottish chroniclers in throwing aside the illegitimate Arthur and setting up Mordred in his stead, the Scots persisted in claiming seniority in the royal line of Brutus.

12. See also Selden's notes, *passim*.

13. John Speed's *History of Great Britaine*, 1611, which was dedicated to James, celebrates James's new title.

14. Part of the refrain originally in Thomas Watson's "Nimphes meeting their May Queene," sung by "six virgins" before Elizabeth at Elvetham in 1591, which was changed from "O beauteous Queene of second Troy" to "O gracious King of second Troy" in Pilkington's *First Booke of Songs or Ayres*, 1605. See *Englands Helicon*, 1600, ed. [Macdonald], 1925, pp. 48–49, 230.

15. P. 55.

16. Sig. [¶7ᵛ].

17. Or William Herbert of Glamorgan.

18. Sig. E2.

19. Sigg. B2ᵛ–B3.

20. *The Ioiefull and Blessed Reuniting the two mighty & famous kingdomes, England & Scotland into their ancient name of great Brittaine*, ca. 1604, p. 80.

21. Pp. 29–30, 44–45.

22. Sig. [G8ᵛ].

23. *The Progresses, Processions, and Magnificent Festivities of King James the First*, ed. Nichols, 1828, II, 271.

24. The same, p. 273. See also allusions in Jonson's masque *Oberon, the Fairy Prince*, pp. 376 ff., as well as allusions in other triumphs, *passim*.

25. See also such collections as John Taylor the Water Poet's *Number and Names of all the Kings of England and Scotland, from the beginning of their Governments to this Present*, 1649.

26. P. 171. Cf. Walter Quin's anagrams written to James in 1595. See p. 179, note 127, above.

27. "Dryden's *Albion and Albanius* (1685) shows perhaps a last flicker" (Parsons' footnote).

28. "The Trojan Legend in England," *Modern Language Review*, XXIV (1929), 407–408.

29. The attack on Polydore continued, as is evidenced by "*An vnmasking of Polydore* Virgils *subtilties in discrediting the* British *story*," Ode IV, Canzone xvi, in William Slatyer's *Palae-Albion*, 1621, p. 105. But Geoffrey of Monmouth came more and more to be questioned. See, for example, John Hayward's words to the reader (sig. [¶4]) prefixed to Sir Roger Williams' *Actions of the Lowe Countries*, 1618, the dedication of which to Bacon is signed "Pe: Manwoode." For the impartial and objective attitude of Wheare, see *The Method and Order of Reading both Civil and Ecclesiastical Histories*, translated and enlarged from the Latin of 1625 by Edmund Bohun, 1685, Section XXX, p. 156. For an excellent summary of the charges against Polydore and for a defence of him, see Burton's manuscript notes for a second edition of his *Description of Leicester Shire*, 1622, to have been brought out in 1641, in *The History and Antiquities of the County of Leicester*, ed. Nichols, 1795–1811, Vol. III, Part I (1800), p. 538.

30. Pp. 35–41.

31. Sig. A3. Lilly refers to the second edition of the *Prophetia Anglicana*, Frankfort, 1608.

32. In *Monarchy or No Monarchy in England*, pp. 38–55. No point would be gained by giving out titles of others of Lilly's works or of divers anonymous works dealing with frayed ends of "prophecies" of Merlin. But see "*Merlin's* Mysterious Prophecy on the fate of *England's* Monarchy," in

The Mystery of Ambras Merlins, Standardbearer Wolf, and last Boar of Cornwal, 1683, p. 4.

33. The original is the novel attributed to De Curli: *Tideric Prince de Galles, Nouvelle Historique*, 2 vols., Paris, Claude Barbin, 1677. An English adaptation of the French came out in 1678: *Tudor, A Prince of Wales. An Historical Novel*, H. H. for Jonathan Edwin. In 1849 Emma Robinson brought out her novel *Owen Tudor* in three volumes, a one-volume edition of which G. Routledge and Co. published in 1857. Sometime about 1600 Drayton collaborated with Anthony Mundy, Richard Hathway, and Robert Wilson the Younger in the drama *Owen Tudor* (*Henslowe's Diary*, ed. Greg, 1904–08, Part I, p. 117). In Roger Boyle, Earl of Orrery's *Henry V*, which is not an adaptation of Shakspere's *Henry V*, the King and Owen are firm friends, and both are in love with Catherine. The play was first acted at Lincoln's Inn Fields on August 13, 1664, with Betterton taking the part of Owen and Mrs. Betterton that of Catherine (Genest, *Some Account of the English Stage*, 1832, I, 53). See also "A Song of the wooing of Queen Catherine by Sir Owen Tudor, a young Gentleman of Wales," printed together with the music in Edward Jones's *Musical and Poetical Relicks of the Welsh Bards*, 1794, pp. 130–132.

34. University Library (Cambridge) MS. Ee. 3.53.

35. Ff. 3–3ᵛ (unnumbered).

36. Ff. 7–7ᵛ (unnumbered), pp. 1ff.

37. Pp. 191 ff.

38. Pp. 379 ff.

39. Ff. 7–7ᵛ (unnumbered). Each book has its introductory stanzas, and is divided into twelve cantos. The Spenserian stanza, of course, is used throughout.

40. F. 5ᵛ (unnumbered).

41. Bodleian MS. Rawlinson Poet. 28. See H. E. Rollins, "Samuel Sheppard and his Praise of Poets," *Studies in Philology*, XXIV (1927), 509–555. The poem was completed in Newgate about May, 1650, and revised "almost foure yeares."

At one time I was engaged in preparing for print a Spenser

continuation-volume which was to include Sheppard's *Faerie King* and the *Supplement* that for a long time was attributed to Robert Jegon. See the preface to this edition.

CHAPTER VI

1. Consult especially R. H. Fletcher, *The Arthurian Material in the Chronicles*, 1906; J. E. Wells, *A Manual of the Writings in Middle English*, 1926, with several supplements; and R. S. Crane, *The Vogue of Medieval Chivalric Romance du.ing the English Renaissance*, 1919. Special attention should be called to the fortunate digression made by the author of *The Complaynt of Scotlande, ca.* 1549, and to the library of Captain Cox, the Coventry mason. See also "The Library of Mary Queen of Scots, and of King James the Sixth," *Miscellany of the Maitland Club*, 1833–47, I, 3 ff. The reference in *A Veue of the Present State of Ireland* to Sir Lancelot, who "wore the sleve of the fayre mayd of Asteroth in a tourney, whereat Quene Guenouer was much displeased" (Grosart *Spenser*, IX, 100), may allude to the story as told either in Malory's *Morte d'Arthur* or in the stanzaic *Morte Arthur*, a copy of which was in the possession of one Robert Farrers in 1570. See *Le Morte Arthur*, ed. J. D. Bruce (Early English Text Society, Extra Series, LXXXVIII), 1903, p. vii.

2. *Faerie Queene*, IV, iv, 21:4. Spenser's recognition of the famous ballad should therefore be added to that of Sidney and Ben Jonson. See *An Apologie for Poetrie*, ed. Arber, p. 46, and Addison, Spectator No. 70, May 21, 1711, in Chalmers' *British Essayists*, 1823, VI, 35.

3. Oxford *Spenser*, p. 619. See Rollins, "William Elderton: Elizabethan Actor and Ballad-Writer," *Studies in Philology* XVII (1920), 224. In a supposed letter to Spenser, Harvey refers to both Elderton and Thomas Churchyard: "And then perhappes not long after uppon newe occasion (an God will) I must be M. Churchyards and M. Eldertons successours tooe, and finally cronycled for on of the most notorious ballat makers and Christmas carollers in the tyme of Her Maiestyes reigne " (*Works*, ed. Grosart, I, 125–126).

4. In 1565–66 Richard Jones licensed "a pleasaunte history of an adventurus knyghte of kynges Arthurs Couurte." "Possibly," says Professor Rollins, this ballad is the same as "When Arthur first in Court," licensed on December 14, 1624, which Professor Rollins in turn equates with that licensed to Edward Alde on June 8, 1603: "The noble Actes nowe newly found of Arthure of the round table." The 1624 entry is identical with the first five words of the first line of Thomas Deloney's "Noble Acts of *Arthur* of the round Table. To the Tune of, Flying Fame," which appears in *The Garland of Good Will*, 1631. See Rollins, *Analytical Index to the Ballad-Entries*, Nos. 2107, 2915, 1951, pp. 183, 250, 169, respectively, and *The Works of Thomas Deloney*, ed. Mann, 1912, pp. 323–326. The ballad, which enjoyed a great vogue, caught the ears of Shakspere, Marston, and Beaumont and Fletcher. Malevole and Monsieur La Writt join with Falstaff in immortalizing it.

5. "Moliant Syr Rhys Ab Tomas, Un O Gynghoriaid Uchav Brenin Harri VII; Ac I Siaspar, Dug Bedford," Ode X in "Y Dosparth II," *Gwaith Lewis Glyn Cothi* (*The Poetical Works of Lewis Glyn Cothi*), 1837, lines 34, 41–44, p. 165. Professor F. N. Robinson has kindly furnished the prose translation (cf. *The Faerie Queene*, III, iii, 48, and Upton's ed., II, 537 ff.). It cannot accordingly be confirmed, however, that Spenser could read Welsh. But Spenser's interest in Welsh is attested to by the five Welsh words in the account of Brutus Greenshield. The words, which do not appear in either the *Brut Tysilio* or the *Brut Gruffyd ab Arthur* and which are wanting in some copies of the first edition of *The Faerie Queene* (II, x, 24: 8–9), were supplied either by Spenser or by some one with a sufficient knowledge of Welsh pronunciation to suit them to the metre. Whoever added the words to the later issue was attempting to give in their phonetic English equivalents the quality of the Welsh vowels and consonants involved. Spenser introduced these Welsh words obviously to give local color to the chronicle history, which places chief stress on the Welsh descent of the Tudors.

6. *Assertio*, 1544, f. 37ᵛ.

7. British Museum MS. Stowe 572 (*ca.* 1590), f. 54.

8. College of Arms (London) MS. Arundel I, f. 73ᵛ.

9. The same, f. 90ᵛ.

10. *Faerie Queene*, III, iii, 44: 5.

11. *The Breuiary of Britayne*, 1573, ff. 65ᵛ, 65.

12. *Faerie Queene*, I, ix, 4: 6–8.

13. *The Breuiary of Britayne*, f. 70ᵛ.

14. The same, f. 13ᵛ.

15. Humphrey Lhuyd's version of Sir John Price's "Description of Cambria," in Powel's *Historie of Cambria*, 1584, sig. A.v.

16. Thomas Churchyard, *The Worthines of Wales*, 1587, sig. D3.

17. *The Blessednes of Brytaine*, 1587, sig. [B4].

INDEX

INDEX